I was born in Winchester – Made in the Royal Navy

Alan C Willis

I was born in Winchester – Made in the Royal Navy

Copyright © 2020 Alan C Willis
All rights reserved.

ISBN: 979-8-6511-3200-3
Imprint: Independently published

CONTENTS

	Acknowledgments	i
1	THE STANDARD 1960'S CHILDHOOD	1
2	SECONDARY SCHOOL AND ONWARDS…	15
3	THE ROYAL NAVY CAME CALLING	24
4	THE MERCURY EXPERIENCE	48
5	FIRST WARSHIP – HMS ARK ROYAL	54
6	USA AND BEYOND	66
7	BACK HOME TO DEAR GUZZ	79
8	BACK AT SEA…	86
9	MERCURY, A REUNION AND A MAGICAL LOAN	93
10	ROYAL NAVY DISPLAY TEAM (RNDT)	101
11	BACK TO CIVVY LIFE	111

ACKNOWLEDGMENTS

I have tried to recreate events, locales and conversations from my memories of them. All stories and events are true, but some may be out of sequence. In order to maintain their anonymity in some instances and as requested, I have changed certain names of individuals and places. I may have changed selected identifying characteristics and details such as physical properties, occupations and places of residence.

Thanks to my Information sources and inspiration:

HMS Ganges Museum
HMS Ark Royal (R09) Communicators
RNA / RNCA
Stuckey, Coxall and Ben
My gorgeous Irish wife
MOD (Navy) for allowing use of the title
Many sources on th'internet

1. THE STANDARD 1960'S CHILDHOOD

I was born in the mid-50s and grew up on the Winnall Council Estate in Winchester. Of course, many pre-age5 memories are sparse, but by the time the swinging 60s arrived, I was off and running, listening to The Beatles and Rolling Stones on pirate Radio Caroline and causing trouble everywhere as I ran riot through adolescence and into my teens.

A family of eight, I was number-3, living in a 3-bedroom council house. It was usual for Dads' to go to work full time, every day in the 60s. Our Dad left the Royal Navy just after I was born in 1955 however, he was then re-called into the RN Reserve for a short time as the Suez war was beginning to rise the headlines again.

Like all ex-matelot Dads, he was keen to resettle after service life, but as a seaman, he had little transferrable skills into the civilian world and initially found it difficult. He did find a job labouring on a building site. He always worked hard and brought home the wages to keep the family. I was the youngest of three at that time, but there were three more siblings to come as the Willis family grew. At some point his luck would change at the building site, and when the digger driver went off sick, Dad managed to persuade his boss that he could fill-in and do the job on a temporary basis. This was great preparation for a full-time career as a digger driver (or Plant Operator if you want to bring it up to date with modern titles). Dad went on to work for some of the big construction giants like Costain and McAlpines, and eventually became a plant demonstrator for RMC Plant Group driving Ford and JCB diggers.

As for our Mum, she worked part time in many different jobs from packing sausage rolls at the Brasils Foods factory in Winnall, to office cleaning, and many jobs in-between; which proves the fact that in the 60s kids actually, were left on their own at times. Both our parents grew up in 30s and 40s and lived through post-war rationing, so most parents were very thrifty and liked to make the money spread as long as it could. We were always fed well and the basics of bread, meat and vegetables was our standard diet; Dad would often go out shooting with Mum's brother, Uncle George, and sometimes bring home a rabbit or a pheasant which was cooked up for a Sunday feast. Most weekends our Mum would buy a joint of meat from the butchers on a Friday – cook it on a Saturday, keeping the dripping. Sunday, she would slice the meat and place it into the roasting dish with the dripping and sometimes an Oxo cube, then we'd have a lovely Sunday roast. The leftover meat was usually made into a shepherd's pie on Monday or Tuesday. Mum was infamous for overcooking the vegetables, so most of us hated eating slushy cabbage and super soft carrots, but Dad would often keep us at the table until the plates were clean. It was quite usual for me to be left there, sat alone at the dining table with a pile of cold cabbage soaked in greasy cold gravy, definitely avoiding it. I think this is where the general revulsion of vegetables cropped into the lives of all of us siblings, we all grew up hating most things vegetable, except for the odd can of processed peas. Sometimes, if there was dripping and jelly left over, we would have this on bread or toast during the week too – lovely with a sprinkle of salt.

As a family, we would all sit together to eat Sunday roast, but we almost always had a quiet table. Dad would not like anyone to speak at meal times, and often kept a stick on the table to rattle your knuckles if you spoke out of turn. Dad also loved his full english breakfast on a Sunday so we would all enjoy this too and we all loved Sunday tea because this was the only day, we could have real butter – on weekdays we had Stork margarine on our bread. Mum spent most of Saturday baking cakes as this was an easy and cheap way to feed the eight us during the week. Usually a victoria sponge, sultana cupcakes and sometimes she would splash out on ingredients and make a ginger bread or a lemon meringue pie, but her speciality was to use the old stale bread and produce a wonderful Bread Pudding. These memories have turned into a modern Willis family tradition and even today, my kids and I like to bake cakes. This fond memory has also kept bread pudding in my diet to this day.

Our Mum loved knitting too, so all of us kids had a knitted jumper for every occasion. This was good for Mum and Dad's budget, but for us it proved a little embarrassing at times. When I started school, all the kids had the new school uniform – I had Mum's knitted version. When I joined the Cubs all the kids had new uniform sweaters – I had a knitted green jumper. Growing up, and as Mum got better at knitting, she would try doing all kinds of fancy stuff. All of us had a great collection of motif cardigans too – footballers, motorcycles, horses, dogs – you name it. Mum is still at it today – aged 87. We each had a fancy Aran jumper for Sunday best (usually off-white in colour, with cable patterns on the body and sleeves) that we could all wear to church. Dad was confirmed in the Church of England and so it followed that we were brought up as CoE christians too, and regular church or Sunday school was Dad's way of forcing the religion on us. To be fair, we needed those thick woollen jumpers especially during the very severe winter of 1962. Our school was closed because power lines were down, roads became blocked and Winchester became gridlocked for days. During most winters we would all huddle around the only coal fire to keep warm and go to bed with a ton of blankets so heavy that you hardly move. Waking up in the freezing cold was an absolute nightmare - it was so cold that the frost would form on the inside of the bedroom windows, so getting out of bed and changing for school with your teeth chattering was not always good experience.

Families and friends were very close back then and stood up for each other no-matter what, so my brother Mick had no choice, but to take me to the pictures on a Saturday morning, much to his disgust, but he would always look after me and introduced me to his mates as "titch". He was always very patient with me too; I can't recall any times when we fought - as siblings we argued occasionally, but never actually had a fight. He was even patient with me when, following one of our sibling disputes, I threw his entire box of Scalextric down the stairs and pulled the wires out of the controllers.

The Odeon cinema was one of two cinemas in Winchester (the other was the Theatre Royal, known locally as 'The Flea Pit'). I often went to Saturday Club at the Odeon – admission 6p (that's just 2½p in today's money) but eventually I got a job as a Kids Club Marshall. This meant trying to keep the other screaming kids under control – but was free entry for me (and my mates). Mick did take me to the Odeon to watch the 1966 FIFA World Cup Final highlights. This was the first football match played at Wembley Stadium. The match was contested by England and West Germany, with England winning 4–2 after extra time to claim the Jules Rimet Trophy. It was the first - and to date, the only time that the England team has hosted or won the World Cup and will always be remembered for the only major international title - and of course for Geoff Hurst's hat-trick. We watched the match live at my mate's house, but this was the film documentary called 'Goal!' – or something similar.

5-year-old me – first school photo

My older sister Sue, and my brother Mick had a two mile walk to Highcliffe Estate to attend All Saints School but I was lucky as by the time I was 5 years old, in early 1960, Winnall estate had the new primary school built – just in time for me to go there. It was September 1961 when I was taken to Winnall County Primary School for the first time. I will always remember parts of that first day as Mum dropped me to Class-1 with Mrs Ersill. I was terrified! After Mum said goodbye, I managed to get free and run out of the school gates after her. I have few memories of Winnall School – like sports days when the red team always won, or securing my place in the school football team. Also, remembering the PE Lessons in the school hall. This was a voice on the Radio from 'The Schools Broadcasting Corporation'. I think it was called something like 'Music, Movement and Mime' where the teacher would say, "children I want you to be a tiny seed, and grow into tall plant and sway in the wind". This was usually in bare feet, vest and shorts – or in our pants if we forgot to bring the PE kit. The poor girls would have to do the lesson in their knickers too!

All the street kids would often meet for fun, games and frolics 'on the street', but we also spent time with each other's families. I spent a lot of time at Heathy's house, or at his Nans who made fabulous scones every time we went there. One day we were all looking forward to a birthday party at Nige's house, so at the allotted time, the alarm came for us all to go home to get washed and changed for the party. When I got back home, the doors were locked, which was very unusual for our street. I knocked on the doors and started shouting for someone to let me in – but no one did. I went to the front of the house and started knocking the window. Still no one answered – so I started banging, louder and louder – when still no reply, I head-butted the window which smashed the glass. Well, that certainly woke everyone up BUT I ended up in bed with a sore arse and I never did make Nige's birthday party. My Dad often said that a fair punishment to suit the crime was all that was needed. In retrospect, I think Mum and Dad were probably 'moving the furniture' when they locked me out so not to be disturbed!

I hated school and was often in trouble with the teachers. Misbehaviour in school always meant being slapped across the legs, or spanked on the backside. There was one teacher at Winnall Primary who would often slap my legs so hard that my skin became dark red and raised. Others would rap your knuckles with a ruler, or slap you across the arms. Corporal punishment was common in those days, and got even worse at Romsey Road Boys Secondary school.

The family couldn't afford a television so most days kids played on the streets with friends. I had a great group of mates from my Winnall days, and I would hang around with a number of different groups – now here's a few nicknames of the usual suspects; Buggy, Ding-a-ling, Housey, Heathy, Nige, Rob, Jimmy, Meach, Nunny and a few others. Between us, we got up to all kinds of shenanigans, from climbing trees and scrumping apples to throwing stones at cars from the bridge over the Winchester by-pass. We would play football in the streets, or we'd steal building material from the local builder's yard or from the tip, and make 'secret dens', or manufacture bogey trollies out of a plank of wood and some old pram wheels and race them down hills. We even built one with a polythene roof, I think it was modelled on Fred Flintstone's car, but that one fell apart on the first downhill run. Our favourite pastime was to collect bike parts from the dump and build off-road bikes for the mud track. I like to believe that we were so far ahead of our time that we inadvertently invented BMX, although strangely, that phenomenon did come along in the 70s anyway. I also remember finding my first batch of porno mags down the dump – a Parade and a couple of Men Only magazines - wow! We did get a television at some point, as I remember racing home from school to watch the new TV soap 'Crossroads' which started at 4pm - the first show after ITV started broadcasting for the day.

On the weekends, we had to fill our lives with something

else to do. In the summer months we would often spend most our time at the Winchester Lido outdoor pool. Mum would just pack us off with a tanner to get in, and another for a cup of hot Bovril for lunch. If the weather wasn't good, we would travel to Southampton indoor swimming baths. It was quite normal that Lynchy's Mum would give me the money for the train ticket. Sometimes we would leave early in the morning and only come home when the street lights came on that evening – that's one long day out. The rule from Mum and Dad was when the street lights come on, you must get home.

In the 60s and 70s any group of children who were disobedient, emotional, and uninhibited were seen as 'naughty disruptive kids' and most people simply blamed these behaviours on biology. Early theories were that these children were the victims of poor parenting, and more discipline was the best treatment. Thinking back, I would have been categorised as one of those kids and as having 'attention deficit hyperactivity disorder' (ADHD) or 'attention deficit disorder' (ADD) as it's known today, but these were never heard of as a diagnosis back then. I was just branded a very naughty boy. My Dad wouldn't have believed those theories anyway as he was always very strict on us all, and particularly on me as I was often the cause of an upset between Mum and Dad – and could often be found in bed with a sore arse. Mum would often sneak a plate of sandwiches up the bedroom for me so I didn't miss tea, much to Dad's disappointment.

There was one occasion when I found myself confined to my bedroom for something or another, but I just got so bored sitting there doing nothing. I was never a reader, but I did have the occasional secondhand comic from my brother's collection of Topper for Kids. Getting bored always led to me getting into trouble and this day was no different. In the bathroom, I discovered one of Dad's discarded razor blades and I thought I might examine just how sharp they really were. I took the blade to my bedroom and lightly touched the mattress. I was fascinated to see how the material sprung apart so quickly, I just had to try it again.

I was so excited by the reaction, I had to try it again on Mick's mattress, and then Dave's. I was having great fun until I stopped and realised just what I had done. Oh my god, how was I going to hide this from Dad! Of course, I couldn't and that same afternoon, I got the thrashing of my life with the buckled end of Dad's belt. My arse was so sore, I could hardly sit and it felt like I was crying all night long. That night, I didn't get a plate of sandwiches from Mum.

Dad was always very firm with us and when he took the belt to me and smacked my arse, I didn't hate him nor did I develop any trust issues; I just respected him and knew my boundaries but was never actually scared. I knew that if I pushed the boundaries too far, like the mattress incident, the likelihood of a good belting was going to be the outcome. Mental health was not even considered in the 60s and 70s, as kids generally didn't have anxieties or personality disorders, we just got on with it or got a slap from our teacher, or parent or the local bobby. I think this was the start of me becoming a Mummy's boy!

1965 – aged-10

Paying attention has always been my downfall, with all of life's distractions – other kids, siblings, toys, television, that little dare to do something more exciting albeit often naughty, or just an inkling that it might be more fun or more rewarding; If anyone was going to throw a pencil at the school teacher, or blow rice through a pea-shooter at the bus conductor, it was always going to be me. I never suspected I might have some type of learning problem, as I was just an average child at school even though (I thought) I worked hard in the classroom. I would often spend two to three time longer than most in the class trying to understand the sum or the spelling. I just couldn't understand the reasoning behind why I was more interested in things other than academia.

Mum found a way to fight this naughtiness and enrolled me into the Wolf Cubs and of course, she had knitted me a green Cubs uniform jumper. Joining the Cubs was the best decision ever as I was 'allowed' indeed encouraged, to run off steam, climb trees, pitch a tent in a field and hike through the mud. I loved the outdoors and really looked forward to the summer camping each year. We used to go to a field near Meonstoke – and spent the week playing games, peeling spuds, assembling rope bridges, building and sleeping in bivouacs, cooking, learning badges and running through the muddy river at the bottom of the camp site. The evening often ended by building camp fires and singing songs with a barbecue and hot chocolate.

I was really lucky one year, to go camping at Gillwell Park – the home of Scouting, the park is famous throughout the world for its Scouting heritage, beautiful setting and stunning range of activities. The Wolf Cubs was so me - I was promoted to Sixer, I earned the Leaping Wolf badge, I had two silver stars in my cap, and endless endeavour badges.

I remember my very first summer camp at Highcliffe-on-sea. Thursday was parents visiting day – and although I was having the time of my life, seeing Mum was so emotional I had to fight back the tears to stop being embarrassed in front of the others. One of my proudest moments was leading my Cub pack and carrying the Standard of the 12th Winchester Green Jackets Wolf Cubs at the front of the St Georges Day parade through Winchester High Street. I also went on to become a Boy Scout and patrol leader of the Peewits.

The big news in 1969 was being woken early by my Dad so I could come downstairs to watch Apollo 11 make the first landing on the Moon. Commander Neil Armstrong and lunar module pilot Buzz Aldrin formed the American crew that landed the Module Eagle. Armstrong became the first person to step onto the lunar surface six hours after landing and Aldrin joined him later. They spent more than 2 hours together outside the spacecraft, and they collected lunar rocks to bring back to Earth. Pilot Michael Collins flew the Command Module alone in orbit while they were on the Moon's surface. Armstrong and Aldrin spent a total of 21 hours on the moon surface at a site they named 'Tranquility Base' before lifting off to re-join the orbit and a successful return to earth for the spectacular splashdown. The 60s was dominated by the US and the Vietnam War, Civil Rights Protests, and also witnessed the assassinations of US President John F Kennedy, his brother Senator Robert Kennedy in Los Angeles and Martin Luther King, but finally ended on a good note when the Apollo 11 landed on the moon and returned home safely.

The family didn't have many highlights, but from memory, one came along every few months when the electricity and gas board sent their collectors round to the house to empty the meter. We were fascinated to see the guys empty the coin tray onto the dining table, and count the cash inside, hoping for a rebate. The guys would just count the cash in front of us as we watched them go so fast as they slid the coins into the cupped hand as they counted, then leave the money in piles. The electric box was full of shilling pieces, whilst the gas box had half-crowns inside. If we were really lucky, Mum would get half-crown (two shillings and sixpence) or 15p in today's money, as a rebate, or a few bob from the electric.

Our social life as kids was simply street football or bikes: We would visit other people's houses to play with toy cars, or soldiers or we would all crowd into someone else's home if they had a television. In January 1965, all the kids in the street went home to watch the funeral of Sir Winston Churchill which was broadcast live on the BBC and seen around the world. It was the first state funeral of a politician in the century. This was exciting for us young lads, especially for an influential lad like me to be able to watch the Royal Navy given the great honour of carrying and escorting the coffin on a Field Gun and limber carriage. This memory was now locked into my brain.

The 'local' football team was always Southampton who played in the second division. My brother Mick was a big Saints fan and used to spend time at the Dell. The stadium hosted first Division football for the first time in the 1966-67 season and was well known for attracting large crowds. I remember going to see Saints play Manchester United in 1969 where we were crammed in so tightly, as a young lad I didn't get to see very much of Bobby Charlton and George Best but I understand that the crowd capacity record was broken that day with over 31,000 people. The game had an unfortunate ending that day as United beat the Saints by 3-0. Saints had a great team back then, with big names like Mick Channon, Ron Davies, Terry Paine, Hugh Fisher and big full-back David Webb. Saints performed well in division2 and reaching the quarter-final stage in the newly created League Cup in 1961. They eventually earned promotion to Division One in 1966.

Back then, plastic bottles and single use plastics in supermarkets were never seen. It was all glass that were all recycled and reused. We used to walk the streets knocking doors and asking people for their fizzy drinks and old beer bottles which we could take back to the pub, or the shop, so we could collect the deposit – sometimes tuppence for each one (that 1p in today's money). We didn't have plastic carrier bags as all loose food was put into brown paper bags, even the new supermarkets (Macfisheries in Winchester) were using brown paper bags. All sweets were bought in 1/4lb and put in a paper bag. My Mum used to carry heavy shopping bags or used a linen bag. We all walked to school from 5 years-old, not jumping into Mum's latest 4x4. We had no fast food, McDonald's or Burger King, no plastic 'happy meal' toys, no polystyrene food boxes to litter the streets with, we had yesterday's newspapers to wrap our fish and chips. Our milk was delivered at 5am 6 days a week by a milkman who drove an electric vehicle! Holidays were almost always here in the UK – we used to have days-out, where we would all pile into the back of Dad's van and head to Hayling Island or West Wittering for the day, or sometimes even to the New Forest for football, kite flying and a picnic. We couldn't afford to fly to far off destinations? We didn't have mobile phones and tablets, so the UK didn't have to import batteries or mine cobalt. This should remind today's generation to take a peek in their [recycled] mirror and re-think if it was really my wasteful generation who are screwing up the planet.

School summer holidays were great as I enjoyed the sunshine and the big outdoors. One of my Winnall school mates lived with his parents and 4 brothers on a farm near Easton. Strangely the name of the farm was 'Shoulder of Mutton' – strange because the family looked after a dairy herd of Friesians, so no sheep! Back in the summer of '65 (yes, there is a song about that) I spent every single day of the 6week school holidays at the farm. I learned so much about the place; watching the daily milking sessions; helping to clean the dairy after milking and shoveling the cow shit out after the session. I also learned not to get too close to the cows when they were in the parlour as I managed to get a swift kick in the shins – and that hurts. I also witnessed for the first time, calves being born and how sometimes, the mother needs a helping hand with the delivery. The farmer would tie strings to a stick, and with his foot as leverage, he would pull the calf out. I would also help to collect eggs from the henhouse, but then got into a bit of trouble with feeding the hens on seed barley. The farmer wasn't too happy with me. I really enjoyed helping with the summer harvest and sitting on the back of the bail sledge being towed by the tractor. We would sit and chat whilst the bailer did the work, then when we had 10 bails, we would open the gate, slide out on top of the straw, and build a stack. This made it easier for the farmer to finally collect them with the trailer for off-loading into the barn. We have great fun in the barn too – as we stacked, we would build tunnels, so when harvest was over, we would have time to play in the barn and re-discover the tunnels. One day, we were all trying to hit tin cans off the wall using home-made catapults, but none of us were very good at hitting the targets, but we kept trying. On one occasion the brothers suggested a new target, but this idea was probably based on our lack of hitting the cans off the wall. I was dared to attempt to smash the glass window in a chicken house. As requested, I picked up a pebble, loaded the sling and fired at the window. SMASH! Unfortunately, this made me the villain again as the farmer was not very happy with me and I got zero support or protection from the brothers.

I often reflect that the 'swinging sixties' was a wonderful time to grow up with a proper family life, where everyone in the street knew you and your parents, and everyone respected you and your families. Even the local Bobby PC Les Pearce, would know who you were; he knew my Dad well as he would be constantly reminding him to put the parking light on the van in the street. Dad would use an old oil lamp, the type you saw on a building site, or road works.

Overnight parking lights have long since been abolished but it was on offence back then if you missed it. PC Pearce would often give me a clip around the ear if I misbehaved too, but as an ex-sailor himself, he would also share stories of being in the Royal Navy.

60s school was great too - proper hearty school lunches and free school milk, visits to the school from the nit-nurse and dentist and fabulous stories of old school days and, I remember when not everyone made it into the school football team (just imagine the parents complaining if that happened today). The 60s also saw the UK's large campaign 'I'm Backing Britain' encouraging everyone to buy British, and we even saw success at winning the Eurovision Song Contest with Sandie Shaw (Puppet on a String 1967) and Lulu (Boom Bang-a-Bang 1969) – but that's before the contest became too political – and rubbish!

2. SECONDARY SCHOOL AND ONWARDS…

Romsey Road had a terrible reputation and the stories that came about were quite frightening for a young lad, so in my defence, I believe that I wasn't naughty, I was simply adjusting myself to the requirements of being a Romsey Road boy. However, the school was to change in a big way with the appointment of a 'super head' – a former Army Officer who had served in El Alamein with the Desert Rats. He updated the behaviour policy, changed the school uniform, improved the homework, he removed some of the old teachers and invited his ex-Army boss to rename the school. A very famous Field Marshall came and officially opened the new 'Montgomery of Alamein' school. The Headmaster was very strict in all ways. I can remember being caned and belted by him; hit across my backside with the science teacher's galosh and being knuckled on the head by an ex-boxer history teacher. One maths teacher would slipper your arse with a plimsole with a golf ball inside – ouch! Sometimes I considered it was better to be caned by the headmaster (he would give six of the best across your hands) than the deputy headmaster (who would give you six of the best across your bum). The latter was much more painful.

To be fair, I didn't really help the situation either. I was actually labelled in the first year of Secondary School when on a school music trip to London, I was responsible for exploding some stink bombs in the Royal Opera House. I was caned live on stage, in front of the whole-school assembly the next day, and banned from all school trips for life – and I was only 11 years old. Of course, I couldn't share this at home because Dad would simply belt me again. It took years before my older brother told me that I didn't need to bribe him anymore. The arguments still go on today about punishments of this nature. I would just say that it was character building.

Starting at secondary school was a whole new encounter as one experiences the fall from the tough senior at primary school, to the lowest junior at secondary. The senior school curriculum was very different and it employed streaming. With streaming, pupils are assessed for their general academic abilities, and put into classes accordingly. That class stays together for all subjects throughout, and may be re-streamed at the end of each academic year. My brother Mick was placed into C-stream, and to provide him with a terrific laugh, I was placed into F-stream. My Mum and Dad knew this was probably the right level for me as my tendency for poor concentration and capacity to be distracted all the time, meant I was always going to be more hands-on than academic. School classes in the 60s were usually 30+ pupils, only one teacher and with no classroom assistants. You either 'got it' or you didn't – there was no help, no special needs nor special assistance – and if you didn't 'get it', it was tough luck, move on.

As an introduction to the new stricter style of Mr Beacham and his management team, I remember our first whole-school assembly. With the new Head came investment in school infrastructure with many upgrades including repainted corridors and classrooms, and refurbished toilets which someone had graffitied already. Mr Beacham stood on the stage and spoke very clearly, saying "in your eyes I may well be a fu*king twat, but you don't need to write on the toilet walls".

For me, secondary school meant meeting the older boys and hearing new things. Learning how to use the fantastic new collection of four-letter words and how to smoke properly by actually inhaling. Smoking became the norm because it made you look tough and like a movie star – usually spending the money your mum would give you for school dinners, on cigarettes. I recall being able to buy a pack of 5 Park Drive cigarettes for just a shilling – that's 5p in today's money.

I often looked for other ways to make money and from my trips to the dump, I would bring back old planks of wood to cut up, and axe them into kindling for fires. I would fill a paper carrier bag with wood and sell door-to-door for a shilling. In another idea, I knock on doors and ask people for old clothing to sort into rags. The Rag and Bone man would pay a few Bob for 10lb bag of rags – but a little bit more if you separated the wool from the rest. Sometimes I would take several sacks of rags at a time. The easiest way to make money was to sell Mum's bread pudding at school, or sitting outside the pubs in Winchester High street singing 'Penny for the Guy' on the build up to Fireworks day. Other money-earning opportunities came and went, so when the council were extending the housing stock into Firmstone road at Winnall, the plasterers offered to pay me half-crown (2 shillings and 6d) per house if I swept the floors and cleaned after them. This was dirty and dusty work, involving every room in the house, and plastering was very messy. I just swept the rubbish into piles, shoveled it all up and threw is all out of the windows.

One of Mum's many jobs was as a 'lady that does' for a rich family who lived in an enormous house on the River Itchen between Abbots Worthy and Easton Village. Mum would do general housework for the lady of the house. The gent was a London City currency trader and the family had a Land Rover and an Aston Martin DB5. The Nanny and the Au Pair would also share an Austin Mini and collected Mum from Winnall every day in this. This led on to another job for me too, cleaning high-end cars. Each weekend, I would rock up with a mate and start cleaning the cars – Hot soapy fairy liquid wash, bucket rinse down with water from the river, and a chamois finish. The gent of the house would give us half-crown per car – usually two cars, sometimes all three. I loved cleaning the Aston and had fabulous daydreams pretending to be James Bond sitting behind the wheel and racing through the streets of Monaco, or somewhere! I think this started my complete fascination of cars which has stayed with me today. It was an easy 5-shillings a week to earn, although the best part of the cleaning routine was, several times a year, the family would host dinner parties, which meant on a Sunday morning, there could be up to 10 cars there. Some of their guests also wanted their cars cleaned, so we would go home loaded with half-crowns and feeling like millionaires. My passion for cars began!

If I wasn't out trying to earn money, I was probably getting myself into trouble. There was one day when I was out and about with mates Buggy and Dinger, where we came across an old school house tucked away near the back of the Ritz Bingo hall. The place was derelict and falling down, and the doors had been knocked in, so the place had been gutted. Somehow, we managed to get onto the roof and (I have no idea why) we started to kick what was left of the glass windows through, watching the broken glass fall inside on to the hall floor. This was fun idea, until I miss-kicked and cut my ankle quite badly, on both sides. I knew I had cut myself almost immediately as I felt the blood filling up my plimsole, although strangely, I wasn't really in pain. The boys carried me home whilst we thought up a story to tell my parents. Dad would kill me if he knew the truth, so when home, I told them that I jumped over a wall and landed on a broken milk bottle. Dad took me to casualty at Winchester hospital where they placed stiches into both sides of my ankle. The nurse bluntly suggested that I was lucky not to severe my achilles tendon in the middle.

Around the start of the 70s, the Skinhead culture was starting to build in Britain. The rise to prominence of skinheads came in late 1960s and early 70s. The film Clockwork Orange offered a glimpse into the culture as these first skinheads were working class youths motivated by an expression of working class pride for England, and modelled themselves on close-cropped or shaven heads and working-class clothing such as high rise Doc Martens boots, thin clip-on braces, varying length straight-leg Levi jeans with the half-inch turn-up, and button-down collar Ben Sherman shirts, usually slim fitting in check or plain. I wasn't in any position to afford the high cost of such luxury fashion in those days, but tried to liken myself to the style and at least have my hair cropped. I tried once to wear some hobnail boots in attempt to look tough, but they just didn't work as I clunked myself around the place. Eventually I managed to save enough money for a pair of second hand Doc Martens, Levi's and a Harrington style jacket, but the rest of the gear was way out of my budget range.

As I got older, Friday night was disco night at the King Alfred Boys Club. The club would be open to girls too, and discos became infamous for sneaking in a bottle or two of Newcastle Brown and hoping we were not caught. Sometimes it was better to hide in the car park at the rear of the Ritz Bingo hall, and drink the booze there, either way, we were always in for a good night out. Saturday nights were spent trying to find a pub that would serve 14- and 15-year olds. After walking the streets on Winchester and chancing our arms in many, the two outstanding pubs were The Wykeham Arms behind the Cathedral, or The Staple Inn at the top of the town in Staple gardens. Other lads also managed the only night club in town called the Copacabana Club in St Johns Street – but I actually looked like a 15-year-old so there was never a chance that I would ever get in!

This was the age when girlfriends came into my social life. It seemed normal that when the school bus arrived at the top of Stanmore, all the local girls were waiting for the Winnall bus to arrive. We used to exchange glances and swap stories, and occasionally my sister Janet would try to arrange dates for me and her friends. I did get regular 'notes' from Jane, so we later hooked up and used to meet on Saturday mornings, in town for a cuppa at the Cadena café in the high street. Jane did actually invite me round to her home to meet the parents – which made me very nervy. After a while, Nige and I arranged to meet with Jackie and Sharon which was a much better arrangement. We would sit in the park and chat about everything and nothing. Jackie was well-known in the skinhead fraternity as a 'bovver girl' so she had all the latest fashions, which put me to shame. We didn't last long as a couple, but Nige went out with Sharon for years (and years) and I believe, eventually got married. Once again, my sister arranged yet another meeting – there was a family who lived close by where there was 5 girls and two boys. I was introduced to the youngest girl, Lindy. We had some great fun and a friendship that lasted – well, at least until I joined the Royal Navy.

During the early 1970s, many of the boys from our school were joining up with the local Army cadet unit, and I heard that they were about to go off on a 2-week training camp to Wales. Perhaps I thought this would be similar to the Cubs or Scouts camp, or perhaps it was just the ADHD/ADD kicking in again, because I really wanted some of this action. Two of the lads, Fred and Paul-W suggested that I was too late to join, but I managed to persuade my Mum and Dad that I should go on this camp. They thought it was a little strange as I was very into the Royal Navy (and it was my brother Mick who was already in the Sea Cadets), but they gave me the 5-shillings and they got rid of me for two weeks. I had just joined the Hampshire Regiment Army Cadet unit in Winchester!

The Sennybridge Training Camp is a UK Ministry of Defence military training area in Powys, Wales. It consists of approximately 31,000 acres of Ministry of Defence land. The military training area is the third largest military training area in the UK and is in the north of the Brecon Beacons National Park and attracts the UK's elite SAS fighting forces as their own training area.

We were off, but first I had to learn a few things, like basic drill and how to dress (although spare uniform was very sparse). When we arrived there, we discovered that the accommodation was some old pre-war wooden huts with bunk beds. The only heating was a small stove in the middle, but as it was summer, these were not allowed to be lit. We started our training the next day – running around fields carrying a heavy Lee–Enfield .303 rifle, a bolt-action, magazine-fed, repeating rifle that served as the main firearm used by the military in those days. Of course, no blank ammunition at this point, so if we engaged the enemy, we had to shout 'BANG'.

As the first week went on, were given some instruction and a live firing exercise at the range. We were instructed to hold the rifle firmly, and to pull it into your shoulder to soften the recoil. The first shot felt like it had knocked my shoulder out of joint, so I was very nervous for the next and other rounds. A great experience though, and something that prepared me for the Self-Loading Rifle (SLR) in my upcoming Royal Navy days.

As the mid-weekend break arrived, we were given a little time off for sports and leisure, so after breakfast we had to choose what to do. I didn't make it that far, as whilst in the breakfast queue, a lad from another unit tried to push-in the queue in front of me. Of course, I wasn't happy with that so pushed him out of the line again, but he insisted in getting back in. A little scuffle pursued as we stated pushing each other back and forth when, with my tin tea mug in my hand, I whacked him over the head as hard as I could. The fight was on! Rolling around on the dining room floor, we punched each other until I managed to get up, raise my fist and punched him square in the face. I felt the pain rush into my hand and as it started to swell up, I realised that I had broken something. The fight was broken up by the adults, and I was taken to the military hospital for Xray. When I came around from the general anesthetic, I was told that I had broken a metacarpal in my right hand. The hand was strapped up, which meant 'light duties' for the remainder of the camp. But it wasn't over – that evening as I was sweeping the barrack room floor, the guy from the dining room incident came into our hut with his mates, and started picking on me again. He said that he came to gloat that he broke my hand – of course, we all knew I broke it myself by hitting him. Well, in the scuffle that followed, I swung at him with the broom and hit him across the throat. He, and his mates ran off and they never bothered me again but I did hear that he wasn't well for some time afterwards. Oh, how happy I was to be back home after this camp – but I still had to go to the hospital to have the splint taken off my hand. I left the Army Cadets after the camp.

It was 1971 and the time that I should choose a career so I was interested when the new headmaster created careers lessons and appointed certain teachers as 'Careers Advisors'. Some of my friends were taking trade courses; panel beating, car mechanics, welding, butchery, painting and decorating – but I was different.

After a few meetings with a career's advisor, I was 'advised' that I didn't bother with CSE exams and it might be better if I left school (at 15) and try to get any job I could. He said that I was "useless" and obviously had zero confidence in my abilities for the future. This discussion really wound me up and I became very irritated by his comments. The following week I skived off school for a day to visit the Royal Navy careers office in High Street Southampton where I sat and passed the entrance examination and the required medical. On my return to school, I told the school Careers Master that I was going to join the Royal Navy. When he stopped laughing, he reminded me that I didn't have any educational qualifications and it was unlikely that I would have. He reminded me in his sarcastic way, that I needed to pass the RN entry exam first! I think he was stunned when I told him I had already passed the entry exam and medical, and had already been offered a place at HMS Ganges, the RN Shore Training Establishment at Shotley Gate near Ipswich.

There was no point me staying at school any longer, so I left the following April at Easter time and got myself a job in a local factory, sweeping floors and making the tea, but I knew that this job was merely a holding situation to grab some extra money because in just a few months, I would be off to join up. My Dad served in the Royal Navy, also from a boy seaman at HMS St Vincent. During his service he went on to become a Leading Hand Coxswain and Bo'sun, serving in many ships in his time and finally in the Suez

Canal crisis in the mid 1950's. Since I was a young child, I knew that one day I would follow the footsteps of my Dad, and join the Royal Navy.

My Dad (1954)

I managed to acquire several books and countless magazines about the Navy and also recall, around 1967, the then children's TV show Blue Peter presenter John Noakes, made his ascent of the famous Ganges mast for the BBC's programme in an attempt to emulate the "button boy" who would reach the very top of the mast and stand hands-free with only a supporting lightning conductor between his knees. I so wanted to be 'that boy' and wanted to seize this opportunity to prove to my former so-called school Careers Advisor, that I was better than he thought.

3. THE ROYAL NAVY CAME CALLING

On 7th June 1971 I signed the dotted line and joined the Royal Navy at HMS Ganges and the skinhead culture was about to be bashed out of my head for ever. For decades, Ganges was the first taste of naval life for generations of Royal Navy recruits. It trained boys for naval service until it closed in 1976 following the raising of the school leaving age to 16. It had a mixed reputation in the Royal Navy, both for its reputed harsh methods of training and disciplining boys in order to turn out professionally able, self-reliant ratings and for the professionalism of its former trainees. I was a little scared by the joining information I was handed, as one of the punishments was listed as 'Birching' and read "…a form of corporal punishment with a birch rod, typically applied to the recipient's bare buttocks or to the back" - often referred to by former Ganges boys, as 'cuts'. Thankfully, all forms of corporal punishment were banned by the time I got there so I was going to be safe even though this was an excellent deterrent for me and others.

HMS Ganges is particularly famous for its high mast which all boys under training were required to ascend, at least to the half-moon and for the mast manning ceremonies held whenever a dignitary visited the establishment.

Along with about 200 other lads, we were to become known as 25 Recruitment, then divided into groups and sent to our Mess – the place we would live for the next few weeks as we hunkered down into our new routines. I was now to be known as P123... WILLIS AC and was sent to Bulwark – which was at 35 Mess Benbow Lane. There was another area of Ganges known as the Annexe where new recruits are normally housed, but this was under refurbishment so Benbow Lane was used for new entry boys for this short period.

Bulwark mess introduced me to boys from across the UK and all walks of life. Each of us had our own dreams and we had different ideas of what 'good' looked like. I'd never before met a Geordie, a Paddy, a Cockney, a Jock, Taff or a Scouse, so the different regional accents meant learning new words and phrases. But this was short-lived as the Navy had its own ideas of how we would speak. The 'Rig-of-the-Day' (what uniform to wear) became standard as we were introduced to No1s, No2s, No8s, whites, half whites, white fronts, black fronts, gaiters, white PT, Blue PT – and so on. We didn't just learn what to wear, but how it was worn correctly, how it as washed, dried, ironed, pressed, scrubbed, polished and bulled, and names plates had to be stamped or sewn onto each piece of clothing. At no point before had I ever thought of scrubbing my plimsoles inside and out with a scrubbing brush and dhobi dust, removing the laces and adding a bit more dhobi so they could be cleaned by rubbing them between your hands, drying them on the hot water pipes, then covering them in Blanco whitener.

No1 and No2 uniforms are all built around Royal Navy tradition and is made up of several parts: Bell bottoms (trousers), blue zip top, blue collar, silk, lanyard and ribbons, and a cap with cap tally. The bell bottoms had to be pressed with horizontal lines across both legs. There had to be 7 folds (or 5 if you had short legs) with each fold the opposite of the previous (so fold-in, fold-out, fold-in, etc.) and the distance between folds had to be the same size as your ships 'Station Card'. The 7 folds were to (allegedly) represent the 7-seas of the world. The white rope lanyard was originally used to fire the cannons on board ship, but later adapted to carry a knife. The uniform also includes a black 'silk' – originally a 36inch square handkerchief worn around the neck. This was adapted to the main uniform in the mid-

1800s as a sign of mourning for Admiral Lord Nelson. Later it became folded and re-folded into a narrow strip before being sewn together at the ends, it passed beneath the collar before being held in place by a black bow. The blue collar was blue linen with, around its border, three white stripes to commemorate each of Nelson's great Naval victories at the Battles of the Nile, Ushant and Trafalgar, (and overlooking his fourth one at Copenhagen!). The collar was a masterpiece of engineered tailoring and had to be ironed in a specific way. I recall the instructor saying the easiest way to remember how to press a collar is "two tits and a fanny" – representing the folds. The traditional RN dress may no longer fit the needs of today's modern Royal Navy, but for a Service that, each year on October 21st, still celebrates the death of Britain's greatest naval heroes, the "square-rig" uniform is a link to the past and a constant reminder that, down through the centuries, all of those who have gone to sea in ships are members of that same 'band of brothers'.

New Recruit 1971

One of the most impressive of the kit issues was the Burberry gabardine coat in Navy Blue [Black], a Naval tradition going back many years and, as a contract supplier to the UK Armed Services, almost certainly helped Burberry reach the massive reputation it has today. The long Gabardine in 2020 cost over £2000 and with its now well-known unique Horseferry print lining, is the height of fashion. Interestingly, we rarely wore these as they would be tied with white tape and used to 'dress' the end of the mess during inspections. I do recall that as 25 recruitment (1971) we were [probably] amongst the last to receive the traditional Gabardine Burberry as less-expensive alternatives were introduced.

It wasn't just our clothing that we needed to look after – the whole mess had to be scrubbed clean every day; showers, drying room, bed-space and bed blocks. Each morning we had to strip our beds, fold and blankets in a specific way and produce a 'block' and weave the sheets in between each fold of the blankets. Everyone had to do exactly the same, so they all looked the same, in the same size, and the beds were all in a straight line. There was also a large pot which was used for hot chocolate, or Kai as it was known the Navy. The pot was strangely called a fanny – but in the cold weather, a fanny of hot kai and stickies [buns] was soon to become the norm at stand easy (tea break). The fanny and even the dustbin had to be polished too – I'd never seen a shiny dustbin before – and I think this was probably the first time in my short life that I'd ever had to clean a toilet.

Of course – the toilets are known as 'heads'! We were being introduced to a whole new Navy vocabulary where floors become decks, ceilings became deckheads, walls became bulkheads, washing became dhobi (hence dhobi dust being washing powder). This new dictionary simply grew as you became more experienced so by the time you went back home and met your friends and family, they had no idea what you were talking about.

Here's a few more of the most popular– but for an exhaustive list there are several books about 'Jack Speak'. 'Jack' being the generic name given to a sailor.
- ACKERS: Slang name for money.
- ADRIFT: Anyone or anything that cannot be found when it is wanted.
- MASTER: The Master-at-Arms – the Fleet Chief Regulator (Navy Police)
- BANYAN: a party or barbeque on-shore

- BLUE LINERS: RN Cigarettes
- DHOBI: Laundry (Dhobi dust is Washing Powder)
- JIMMY-THE-ONE: Ships 1st Lieutenant
- CHIEF BUFFER: Nickname for Jimmy-the-One's right-hand man
- DIG IN: Common slang for "Help yourself" (to food)
- THE OGGIN: Maritime slang name for the Sea
- PUSSER: slang for a Purser; a ship's supply officer or Paymaster (or a brand of Navy rum)
- SLOPS: name for any article of clothing or the clothing store
- ANDREW: Nickname for the RN used by all ranks
- OPPO: Your opposite number – good mate / best friend
- CHOGEY DHOBI: The Chinese Laundry
- CLUB SWINGER: PT Instructor
- ASHORE: Anywhere that's not onboard (even in a shore establishment)
- STERN: the back end of the ship
- BOW: The front end of the ship (or the pointy end)
- PORT / STARBOARD: Left / Right (Red / Green)
- SCRAN: Food – Often referred as Big Eats

These early days and weeks taught me how to look after myself and keep myself clean and fit. Coming from a family of 8, back home it was often difficult to get a slot in the bathroom when hot water was available. There was no shower at home either, so taking a bath was usually a once-a-week occurrence, but in the Navy, it was frowned upon if you didn't shower every day – and sometimes, twice or more, every day. Mind you, the amount of physical exercise we did every day, we needed a shower once/twice/three times a day. I learned to shower and rinse properly, about deodorant and antiseptic, both of which I never seen before. We were instructed on how to fend off 'Chogey Toe Rot' (athletes' foot) and 'dhobi rash' (jock itch) and so the term 'Bath & Dhobs' was now permanently embedded into my head. We were given presentations about sexually transmitted diseases and how to avoid these, and offered free condoms if you asked (no-one ever asked). Pretty scary for a bunch of 15-year-old virgins! There were occasions when we were all ordered to go and have 'a scrape' (a shave) – something we felt wasn't necessary at such a young age when you had soft fluffy skin, but you always did as you were told, right? - even the light vellus hair (bum-fluff) had to come off. There were several cuts and scrapes, and lots of blood that day. If you didn't keep yourself and your kit clean and tidy, you were deemed to be a 'crab'. One lad in our mess came back from a day's training to find the entire contents of his locker in the dustbin, sitting in the shower room filled with soapy water. This would force him to clean everything again and would take forever. Of course, a very important lesson to be learned quickly by us all. Nobody wanted to be deemed 'crabby'.

Keeping everything clean was also a costly exercise: As a junior, our pay was just £3/fortnight – of which you needed to keep buying toothpaste, shampoo, deodorant, dhobi dust and boot polish. Some of us also had to 'chip-in' for extras for messdeck cleaning, like buying Red Cardinal polish for the quarry tiles on the floors in the showers and toilets. This wasn't provided, so if you wanted to be with even a small chance of winning the 'best mess cake' then you just had to pay up. If you had any change left for cigarettes and 'Nutty' (Navy term for everything sweets or chocolate) you were lucky. Some of the boys would run a fag loan service, by giving out cigarettes for a 100% - 500% payback on pay day – *"if you lend me a cigarette, I'll give you 5 on pay day"!*

Part of the new vocabulary was being added to every day. We all learned that people with a common name were called by the common 'nickname'. This wasn't just your average Smudge Smith either; most of us, at some part in our lives have acquired a nickname. That was usually in the school playground when surnames were adapted to make life easier. These youthful nicknames largely lacked any kind the sophistication of the Navy's versions, usually by of cutting surnames in half and adding a 'Y' or an 'S'. However, the Royal Navy takes nicknames to an entirely different level. Yes, it has the obvious ones 'Ali' Barber, 'Mini' Cooper and

'Albert' Hall, but there are dozens which make no sense at all, the meanings having been lost over the many years. Have you ever met a 'Snakey' Blake or 'Tug' Wilson? Here's a few more: Fanny Adams, Basher Bates, Dinger Bell, Buster Brown, Dixie Dean, Bungy Edwards (and strangely, Bungy Williams), Banjo West, Dolly Gray, Pusser Hill, Flapper Hughes, Rip Kirby, Sharkey Ward, Knocker White, Slinger Wood; and plenty more…

Navy food was excellent and not what I was used to back home. Every morning we would have cereals and a full english breakfast. I did hear rumours that missing breakfast was an offence as this was the meal to set you up for the day, although I don't think I ever heard of anyone actually getting charged – not even those who fainted on parade in the hot summer. We always had three hot meals a day, and kai and stickies at stand-easy time. The main meals introduced me to a number of new-found menu options, corned beef was re-labelled as 'corned dog' (a saying I still use today), or 'Babies Heads' (a steak and kidney suet pudding), or 'shit on a raft' (kidneys on toast) or the one that got us all talking was the 'hammy-eggy-cheesy-thingy' – which is just as it sounds and stirs many memories for countless ex-matelots.

After a few weeks in the New Entry Division, we were divided into different smaller groups and sent to the 'main' establishment. The new groups were based on the specific trade training to ready us for specialist training later on. I wanted to be a Radio Operator so was given an aptitude test whilst in the New Entry Division. The test was fairly basic english, and 'tone' testing – there's no point being a RO if you're tone-deaf. I was accepted and sent to Benbow Division, ironically back to 35 Mess, to team up with my 'new' mates in 251 Communicators Class where we embarked on the early training routines. I had become a 'Nozzer' – meaning the newest recruit into the Navy, and I would remain a Nozzer to all those more senior to me, but a term I could now use when a new cohort recruitment came in after me.

This was the time for our official photographs, so a full parade in No1 uniforms to prepare for a whole series of pictures including the official portrait to send home to Mum and Dad. The official photographer was named 'R A Fisk' who won the contract to become the first official photographer at HMS Ganges (in 1938) and stayed until Ganges closed in 1976. Mr Fisk offered a great selection of standard post cards and photographs of the establishment, including the swimming pool, bowling alley, gymnasiums, and was always on hand to take pictures of Divisions, mess games, awards ceremonies and around the establishment itself. There are many ex-Ganges boys out there today who are extremely thankful of the memories these old photographs bring.

Bulwark Mess – New Entry Division

On our first visit to the CMG (dining hall) we noticed that the Chefs were all wearing black armbands. We asked a couple of them why this was, or had someone died – but was told that this was 'Black Tot Day' - a day of commiseration as that date was the anniversary of the Rum Ration being stopped by the Admiralty. The last rum ration was on 31 July 1970 so this date became celebrated across the fleet as sailors were unhappy about the loss of the rum ration. There were reports that the day involved sailors throwing tots into the sea and the staging of a mock funeral in a training camp. The official Admiralty response was "The Admiralty withdrew the daily tot because they were concerned that a lunchtime slug of rum would hinder sailors' ability to operate increasingly complex weapons systems and navigational tools". In place of the rum ration, sailors were allowed to buy three one-half-pint cans of beer a day. Unfortunately, we were far too young and was never going to get a 'Tot' but the 'up spirits' tradition still goes on with RN Veterans today, for reunions and gatherings of 'the old boys'.

There were several stories about HMS Ganges being haunted and the two main poltergeists were 'The Green Gilbert' and 'The Phantom Roof-Walker'. Both were famous for their individual stories, which scared the life out of us juniors throughout Ganges when the stories were told late at night after lights out. I will try to expand here – but this is just the version that I understood as there were several versions of each. The Green Gilbert was an alleged German U-Boat Commander who managed to escape the sinking of his boat and got himself ashore on the beach at Shotley. He climbed the fence into Ganges and found the Laundry building left unlocked. He was wet, cold and knackered, so decided to take shelter for the night inside the laundry. He allegedly fell asleep inside one of the big warm spin-driers. At some point during the night, the lid of the dryer fell down, and the German was spun to death, and the body turned green. Why? – I've no idea – but this guy's ghost now walks up and down Laundry Hill at night! The second apparition is the Phantom Roof Walker who apparently was an RN PT Instructor who was demonstrating to Juniors the methods of climbing the mast. During the climb, he attempted to pass over the Devil's Elbow (this is an upside-down climb around the first platform) when he fell. He was at such a height that he bounced off the safety nets and was catapulted onto the roof of the Post Office. He was killed, and his ghost now runs along the roof of the Long-Covered Way. A strange way to summarise the two stories, and it must be said, that neither story can be collaborated by real facts, but both stories made for some very scared Ganges kids.

The discipline in the main establishment stepped up a gear. Boots were not allowed in the mess and if you were caught, it could mean several days of punishment. If you were late on parade – several more days of punishment. We were taught how to fold our clothing into the same size as the ships book (a manual of seamanship standards and practices) and then place strips of carboard inside the clothing so it presented a flat surface at the front of your personal locker. I say personal – all lockers had to be left open so they could be inspected daily. Boots, shoes and even football boots had to be spit and polished, to a high quality and lined up under the bed each day. If anything didn't look clean and tidy, they were usually emptied onto the floor so you were forced to start again. If the messdeck was deemed dirty, then the evening was cancelled and everyone had to re-clean the whole place.

Our daily routine was tight – up at dawn with the sound of the bugle playing reveille blaring through the Tannoy system. Prep the messdeck, dress your personal space and your locker, get on with the rig-of-the-day and up to breakfast. It became engrained into your head that Daily Orders listed everything you needed to know about the day – what time you would wake up, what time feeding was, where to be and even what to wear. It was seen as an offence if you didn't read daily orders and something that stuck with you throughout your time in the RN. Failure to read these would put you on a disciplinary path. Divisional Officer's morning parade was usually 7:30am and classes started at 8.15am. We would march as a squad to classes, to meals, to the gym – indeed to everywhere.

The weekend schedule was slightly different. Starting on Friday evening, the messdeck had to be scrubbed from top-to-bottom. All metallic (including dustbin and fanny, the copper/brass piping in the toilets and showers, had to be polished with Brasso (or Bluebell); windows cleaned (usually with old newspaper – we didn't have glass polish or Windolene back then); mess decks were scrubbed with wire-wool and detergent, then waxed and buffed, all by hand, and if you had the red cardinal polish, the showers and toilet floor were scrubbed, polished and buffed. Even the outside had to be cleaned, the gardens needed to be weeded, and litter picked, and the stone flower-bed borders painted white. This was stiff competition, as the Divisional Officer would do 'rounds' (inspection) on Saturday morning when the mess was presented. The cleanest Messdeck would win a giant cake, so if you were lucky, the cake was shared that afternoon. Of course, we made our own fun during these cleaning nights, as winning the cake was the best prize – this led to sabotaging the other messes, thus the introduction 'inter-mess wars'. Each mess would storm another, and throw rubbish around, or stamp a boot mark of the floor. Then someone came up with the idea of the 'Sanilav' bomb. 'Sanilav' was a bottle of soda crystals for cleaning toilets. If the bottle was half-emptied, then topped up with water and shaken hard, the plastic bottle would swell to bursting then explode the crystals all over the mess. These became the Friday night menace to be avoided, for all of us.

Saturday PM was for down-time, or organised sports including football, hockey or cross country running or simply climbing up the famous mast.

The mast was around 143ft high including the top cap, known as 'the button'. Climbers would ascend the rope ladder to the first level where you have an option. You could either go under the platform and up through a hatchway, or climb hanging up-side-down around the devil's elbow and directly onto the second stage ladder. The first couple of times, I always chose the option to go under the platform and through the hole. Doing this a few times improved my confidence. I felt the more often I climbed, the easier it might get and I never drifted from my goal of button boy. The second level is known as the 'half-moon'. Most boys were instructed to climb to this level as a vertigo test but this wasn't enforced. I really wanted to do this and one bright day, I summonsed the self-assurance and went for it. The view was absolutely amazing, but there was very little to hang on to, and I pulled on the self-belief in my head, that I could do it. Again, I spent the next few climbs building my confidence and becoming stronger, but I also knew that I couldn't become overzealous and damage the faith I had built up in myself. The next stage was to ascend the small ladder. Some people had named this as 'Jacob's Ladder' – based on the story of the magical 'stairway to heaven' from a dream of Jacob as described in the Bible. I had no intention of going to heaven just yet, but plucked up the courage to get to the top. Once there, the only hand-hold was the mast itself, and by wrapping your arms around the pole, this was the only way to be able to stand on the last platform before the top. It was only about 10 feet above the half moon, but it felt like a lot more than that. I was now standing on the two spikes either side of the mast, referred to as 'the cow horns'. Just 10 feet to go and I was there, so I made an instant decision. I was almost there, so why not give it a go and take the plunge (perhaps an unfortunate phrase at this stage of the climb). Finally, I plucked up the courage and went for it. Imagine a flag pole, painted in brilliant white gloss paint, and a tad slippery. Imagine also the wind whistling around your body and you have nothing to hold onto except this damn pole. If I could just shimmy up about 8 feet or so, I could grab the steel cables that hold the mast in place, and pull myself up to the button. A slip and a slide, and using all the upper body strength I could muster, I managed to get my face up to the button level. I was now 143 feet up, looking at the button which is about the size of an average dinner plate. There is a short steel lightening conductor that I could grab, and if I had any strength left, I might be able to pull my body up, and wrap my legs around the top. It did cross my mind that the conductor might not be strong enough to take my weight, but plenty of other lads have been doing this for many years, so it must be strong, right? I did it – I was now king of the mast and sitting on the top. I was now shaking like a leaf and had no idea what to do next, so just sat there looking around and trying to work out how to get down again. The mast was shaking too as it seemed that every other Ganges boy was also scrambling all over the place. I thought this would not be a good time to stand up and salute, even though my head was telling me otherwise. Then from below, I heard someone shout "stand still" and the mast stopped shaking and everyone on the mast looked up at me. This was the only opportunity to get this done, at least today. I steadied myself, lifted my right knee up and put my foot on the button, then the same with the left, and then stood up, but found it difficult to finally let go of the conductor spike. After a while, I just went for it – I stood, steadied myself and saluted. I was so proud of myself I hurried back down the mast to tell my mess mates what I had done, then rush to the phone box to call my Mum. I really wanted to be the Button boy at a ceremonial, so I spent as much practicing time as allowed to get into the Mast Manning Team, and onto the Button. There were only two occasions annually that Ganges did a full ceremonial Mast manning display – Parents' Day and Admirals' day. I wanted one of them!

Receiving my Mast Manning
Trophy from Captain Ash

Saturday evenings was recreation time and each division had its own 'rec space', a mini-library, pinball machines, table tennis, etc. but most of us headed off to the Gymnasium where they often showed old RN black and white war movies on the big screen. I have lost count of the times I've watched 'We Dive at Dawn', 'The Cruel Sea', 'The Battle of the River Plate', 'Ice Cold in Alex' and many more. This was probably the first time I watched the gorgeous Ingrid Berman and Humphrey Bogart in Casablanca – a movie which is still my all-time favourite and watched hundreds of time since.

Sunday was full Divisions – meaning a Captains parade of the whole ship. We would parade in full No1 uniforms, by messdeck, class and division. This includes a full personal inspection by the Captain and a ceremonial march-pass and salute. There was also a ceremonial guard with weapons, the famous Ganges Bugle band (and sometimes a visiting Royal Marines Band) providing the marching music. After Divisions, we were marched to Church depending on your religious denomination and beliefs, then stand-easy for R&R (rest and relaxation) after lunch and the afternoon.

The weekday evenings were normally filled with cleaning, ironing and boot polishing for the next day, so at bed time we were always ready for a full night's sleep. There was always someone playing loud music, or groups playing cards and boardgames, but lights out was at 22:30 sharp, and the instructors were very disciplined about this. There was often other fun and games after dark, and sometimes the consequences were just not worth it. I remember one night, the duty Petty Officer wasn't in the best of moods, so after lights out he just demanded – "sleep, now"! At that time, someone farted – the whole mess started laughing – the lights came back on, and we were all sent outside, wearing oil-skin wet weather gear over our PJs, but we had to carry our mattresses over our heads too. Once on parade outside, we were instructed to double-march down the Long-Covered Way, turn around and double-march back up again. Then do it again, and again, until we all stopped laughing. Afterwards, we could return to the mess, absolutely knackered and soaked with sweat inside the oilskin coat, make up the beds again, and eventually turn-in for the night. This was common and happened regularly.

There were several different and 'traditional' punishments for us to learn about, and probably the most difficult was the 'Faith, Hope and Charity' test. FHC was a series of three blocks of steps (hence the now infamous names) running down from the main establishment down to the pier. If things didn't go right, or we as a team didn't do well, or for any other reason beyond us – we had to complete the Faith, Hope and Charity and double-march, as a squad, down the three flights and back-up – and then repeat multiple times. There were similar punishment runs that caused equal pain and suffering – one known as the Laundry Hill run, which as the name implies, another run up and down steep hills! These were tough, but served as a warning to make sure we behaved ourselves all the time.

The kit muster was the next thing to learn: every piece of issued clothing (kit) had to be washed, ironed (or pressed) and folded in to the Ships Book size – and folded in a way where your name-stamp was clearly on display. This had to laid out on your bed, or on the floor ready for inspection. Generally, we were told to lay blues on one side, whites on the other, and include everything. Shoes and boots were spit and polish bulled, plimsoles scrubbed and whitened. The inspections could be quite brutal as only the smallest of marks, scuffs or the tiniest bit of fluff, could mean that you had to start over. We were occasionally allowed a 'dirty pile' (or anything that was in-the-wash) but this could be nothing more than one pair of bed sheets, a pillow case, knickers and socks. (Note: the word 'knickers', not pants, was standard for underwear – it didn't mean we were cross-dressers, or wore the female underwear. Other words for knickers included shit-nix, shreddies, skiddies or grundies). The Navy did actually issue underpants, but these were large aertex type Y-fronts, and I don't think anyone actually wore them. Part of the kit issue included a 'housewife' sewing kit which came in handy as we had to keep all our kit in good order, so adjustments, repairs and the worse thing – embroidering our No8 shirt name tags in red silk. One positive was the phrase 'Make and Mend' which in short, meant we would have time to ourselves (on the premise of repairing kit) but M&M became synonymous with an afternoon off.

The training curriculum was varied and interesting most of the time. By class group, we would have several tests...

Swim training and a swim test (obviously a sailor who can't swim becomes a problem and was referred to as the unflattering name 'backward swimmer'). The test involved wearing a pair of overalls, jumping off the high board into the pool, swimming a few lengths, then treading water for five minutes whilst removing your overalls. Simple for some, and some laughs whilst we watched the backward swimmers jumping from the high board wearing a life vest, then the vest smashing them in the face when they hit the water if they didn't strap it on correctly. A steep learning curve for some.

Fitness training, rope climbing, circuit training, vaulting and weights – then beating the shit out of each other in the boxing ring. This was a great test of character as you either beat up your best mate – or got beaten up yourself. There was no boxing style or rules here – it was just plain mad hitting the shit out of each other until the PTI blew his whistle. The PTIs were very strict on safety and smartness too – looking smart in the gym was an imperative, so just to add to the bullshit, we even had to press creases down the front of our PE shorts. We would only be allowed to change out of all white kit into navy blue kits once the whole class had passed a kit test. A great test of team building and learning together! I remember that one of several Gyms had the poem 'IF' by Rudyard Kipling written on the walls – if you did this, and if you did that, and more, 'You'll be a man my son'. A great reminder to all of us boys, and a poem that means so much more today than it did back then when we were just 15 years old.

Drill – how to march, turning, at the double, saluting, handling a Self-Loading Rifle (SLR) and rifle drills. This was often hard work when trying to get the timing right so the whole squad worked exactly together. The punishments were tough (but often funny too). It was normal for mistakes to be repaid by running around the parade ground with your SLR above your head, but I remember, having made a mistake on the parade ground, having to climb and stand on top of a dustbin, with my rifle held above my head and told to shout "I am a wanker" until told to stop. The instructor would often tell me to shout louder because he couldn't hear me apparently. Again, character building!

Maritime studies and general seamanship training were particularly tough, not only on throwing ropes at each other and learning about navigations buoys and lights, but also firefighting, testing your anti-gas respirator (AGR or gasmask) in the gas chamber with CS gas thrown in. This was part of the NBCD tests (Nuclear, Biological and Chemical Defence). For the most part, the chamber was a means to test our ability to operate as near-normal as possible against far worse substances that just CS gas. This training was tolerable to start with but as you were leaving the chamber, the instructor would order you to remove your AGR and shout your name, rank and number before you walk out of the door. Often, you were asked to repeat but by that time the CS Gas had reached your throat and eyes, and the suffering began. CS gas makes you cough, your eyes and nose are streaming and sometimes you just vomit to clear everything out. Looking back – it was just character building with a serious side and some of the stories are quite funny.

We learned how a warship is made up and how you found your way around – so, decks 1, 2, 3, etc., and sections 'A' (bow) to 'nn' (Stern), then odd numbers were Starboard and even numbers Port side. This would mean a lot more once you joined a ship, for example, when I served on HMS Ark Royal later, I lived in 5K1 mess (so deck 5, section K, Starboard side).

For the 'damage control' test, we had to go into a chamber which was a simulated test for a ship's collision and/or damage to the hull, where large volumes of water came gushing into the chamber. The test was to see if the impairments could be patched up or at least, the water flow could be lessened by plugging the holes with mattresses, timber, wedges and anything else you would find on a ship. We discovered that the water was so cold, we all just climbed onto a higher surface and shivered, but of course in a real situation, we would have all drowned. Looking back now, this was very funny and makes me smile, but once again, this was another test with a serious point to make. On this occasion, we all screwed up!

There was a down-side to training for us all. Each of us had left school at the age of 15, many of us didn't have the opportunity to take our CSE exams at school, so we were sent back to school each day for basic Maths and English lessons. This was also a test for our future within the Royal Navy as this would state our readiness and aptitude for promotion at some stage. We were being prepared for the 'Navy Maths and English Test' (NAMET). The pass grade was set to 7 (maths) and 7 (English) – where a 1-1 was excellent and a 5-5 was promotion potential to senior rank material. I scraped through with a 7-6 but as a non-academic, I was happy with that as it meant I had passed, but needed to get a higher grade if I wanted promotion at any point. I was to do the test again later when I joined the warship HMS

Ark Royal.

Specialist trade training started too. As a Radio Operator, we were introduced to typewriters, Morse code and radio voice operations. This is what I was waiting for and enjoyed every minute. Classes were every day and once we had mastered the QWERTY keyboard, our typing speed and accuracy was increased each week. We learned by using a large screen which lit-up with the call for a particular key stroke. We would wear headphones, and the voice would start: "Starting with your left hand, little finger - Hit the key when I say the word 'now': Ready, Q NOW, A NOW, Z NOW (Next finger): W NOW, S NOW, X NOW, …and so on. We soon got used to the voice and started learning fast. After a while, the instructor would place a card over the keyboard so we couldn't look down at what we were doing, then after a few weeks we were completely flummoxed when the voice told us he was going to drop the word 'now'. Next lesson it was just, Q A Z W S X E D C, etc. This just went on until our speed and accuracy was improved – and a smart smack around the back of the head if you made a mistake, or if you looked down.

Learning the Morse code took a little longer, but again the speed and accuracy targets increased each week and were tested regularly. I was just having a lot of fun and didn't take it seriously as I should have. I did struggle to keep concentration on the Morse reception exercise as I was easily distracted by even the smallest noise or a cough, or the instructor walking around the room behind us (probably part of the ADHD coming out) so when the 9th week examination came, I failed the test with a below accuracy target. This was a huge hammer blow to me and I was completely devastated when told that I was going to be back-classed. The worst, most embarrassing and hurtful part was that a formal letter went to my parents to tell them of the news. There was one consolation in that back-class and a re-test would be my last chance! I had disappointed Mum and Dad and I was really distressed by the whole episode! This shattered my dreams and I shed many tears that day feeling ashamed and embarrassed, but I was determined that this would never happen again. This was a short, sharp and painful lesson that being in the Royal Navy also meant that I couldn't mess around anymore, I had to take control of the ADD and start working harder on my concentration effort in order to get the real job with the real career that I so desperately wanted – and I couldn't afford to screw this up again.

I was back-classed to 27 recruitment (271 Comms Class) but this was far better than being sent home as a failure. I took my kit to my new mess in Blake Division, No6 Mess in the Long-Covered Way. There was two of us from 251 who made this backward move. That same day, we said our farewells to our 251 classmates, and took the 'walk of shame' to meet up with our new 271 classmates. 271 Class took us onboard very well, and we were integrated quickly. Indeed, some of the younger boys took our experience onboard and we learned the next stages together. This was also a time to meet up with another guy from Hampshire. Coxall was a Leading Junior, so was in-charge of Blake 6 mess. His family lived in Fleet, a small town near my own home town of Winchester, so this tenuous link with Hampshire brought us together and we have remained friends ever since. We immediately knuckled down and got into the process again at week 5 – so 4 weeks to prepare again for my retake of the 9th week exam. This was definitely not 4 weeks wasted as I spent many hours on the practice Morse keys in the messdeck drying room and many evenings at the Ganges communications school classroom. The 9th week exam came again and I passed the Morse code part with 99% accuracy, the 3rd highest score in the class.

Having passed this and other stringent tests, and working towards the final exams, I was able to de-stress and relax a little. I volunteered, and was accepted into the HMS Ganges Field Gun team, where we trained hard and provided a great display/race to visiting dignitaries. I also managed to secure my place in the Mast Manning Team, and thankfully I hit the shortlist of potential Button Boys. Along with the other volunteers, we were each told to go up to the button, stand and salute, then return for feedback. In my eagerness to get going, I volunteered to go first, but at that time I didn't realise that the wet weather would have an effect on the last bit of the climb – the shimmy up the pole to the top. I did manage the climb, the stand and the salute, but my technique was hampered by the wet and slippery mast (well, that's my excuse). It seems that my slide back down the pole simply dried off the rain ready for the next guy. I did however, manage to get 2nd place – which meant that I would provide the official 'Button Boy' slot for Admirals day – although my preference would have been Parents day so my parents could see me up there. Instead, they saw me standing on the cow horns just below but it was a great honour to be on the button for the visit of an Admiral.

With too much time on our hands, we had lots of opportunity to mess around and get up to mischief. On one occasion, we climbed through the window of the flag store on the main parade ground, and grabbed the signal flags Foxtrot Uniform Charlie Kilo. We connected them to the halyard on the main mast, and hoisted them up to the top, whilst running away. With hindsight, how many communications classes were at Ganges at the time, whom might know the flag signals. A silly thing to do, but filled in some time and forced another good laugh.

It wasn't long before I got myself into real trouble. One of the lads noticed that the ladies in the NAAFI shop didn't bother closing the windows at night. Apparently, he had been monitoring it for a few weeks, and still the same windows remained open. The plan was to climb in, grab a bag full of cigarettes, rolling tobacco, sweets and other goodies, and get out quickly, but he needed a couple of look-outs. Mr Gullible (me) and another guy, saw this as an opportunity to get free stuff, and volunteered as a look-out. The plan didn't work and we were all caught in the act, and placed into the cells. One of the guys was actually half-way out through the window when the Crushers arrived, so zero chance of an excuse and certainly no alibi for us lookouts. The investigation took over all of our time as we were stuck in limbo – the cell-block was a magnet for other lads wanting to rubber-neck and gloat – although some of these guys brought cigarettes as they glared through the windows. For us, it was 'almost' like a badge of honour. It was agreed that me and the other lookout would completely deny any wrong and demanded to be released, but our calls fell on deaf ears and we stayed in the cells overnight. Our DO (Divisional Officer) came and bailed us out the next day as the investigation kicked in. We had spent half the night talking through the options as we prepared to be taken to the Commanders Table. Our mate 'Stuckey' decided to accept all the blame – but then begged the Commander not to be sent home as he declared that his Dad would "kick the shit out of him". Some claim, but I later found out that this would have been a true scenario. This guy today, still remains an excellent 'oppo' (good friend) and this is when I first heard the phrase "Royal Navy friends are real friends forever". We were all placed on No9 Punishment, Stuckey got 14 days and we go juts 7. No9s meant extra duties, extra drill, scrubbing pots in the galley (kitchen), early morning and late-night reporting in different uniforms (No1s, No8s, half-whites, etc.). I feared that this was another time I had let down my Mum and Dad, again - but the nightmare scenario was over and I think No9s punishment was a fair result for all of us.

I always looked forward to going home on leave to Winchester to see my friends and family, but these opportunities were few and far between. Christmas and Summer were the only two occasions allowed so when these happened, we had to make the most of what time we had and I so wanted to have a pint with my mates in the Wykeham Arms. Of course, the Navy would pay for the train journeys and we were given strict instruction on what we were allowed to do, and what we were not. Meeting with old school mates was fun - they were still working on apprenticeships for panel beating, mechanics, welding, butchery, painting and decorating – and couldn't believe the stuff I had been doing and learning. Ironically back home, I never did hear from Lindy very much, but her sister Noreen kept turning up at the front door, and when I got back to Ganges, she would write letters to me. I just ignored them and decided not to write back. The return journey back to Ganges was usually with excitement as you wanted to share your stories of home with your new best mates.

For the most part, Ganges was a fun, exciting and fantastic opportunity for me where I learned so much, and heard many new stories and met some the most genuine and honest guys anyone could ever meet. Perhaps this was just a sign of me growing up! Of course, there were other things I didn't like at Ganges including cross-country running, diving and walking the sea bed – the Harwich and Felixstowe estuary wasn't the best place to climb down the ladder to the seabed and walk in the mud. I also hated 'Cutter Pulling' (rowing) – a Cutter is a small-medium size rowing/sailing boat. The oars were double-banked – that means there were two oarsmen on each seat, with a rowlock each side, a full crew of about 10-12 rowers and a Cox. The test was pretty tough as we all had to row out and around the Harwich Trinity House Lightship, and return. Ganges would often hold Cutter racing days where we had to go the foreshore and cheer on our divisional team. Often, I had no idea who was who but the event did provide for an afternoon of rest and relaxation by the sea.

We had just one more test to pass, which was quite exciting as this was known as 'sea training' where we met the warship HMS Fearless in Liverpool and sailed with her to Portsmouth. This meant three whole days onboard a real Royal Navy amphibious assault ship. Of course, we got up to no good once again and spent the first evening in downtown Liverpool finding our way around the bars. This was my first taste of Chinese food and Bacardi-coke, introduced by our Junior boss, Chris 'Cocker' Coxall.

Onboard HMS Fearless we learned a lot about Maritime ship-to-shore radio and provided us a small taste of what our real jobs might be like once qualified. As a brief introduction for those non-Sparkers - RATT (Radio Automatic Teletype) is a system of three distinct parts connected: the teleprinter, the modem and the radio. The modem is sometimes called the terminal unit (TTVFT) and is an electronic device which is connected between the teleprinter and the radio transceiver. The transmitting part of the modem converts the signal transmitted by the teleprinter to create a pair of audio frequency tones using Frequency Shift Keying (FSK). On reception, the FSK signal is converted to the original tones by mixing the FSK signal with a local oscillator called the BFO or beat frequency oscillator. At the receiving end, these tones are fed to the demodulator part of the modem, which processes them through to recreate the original signal. The original RATT system speed is based on the maximum operation tempo of the teleprinter using the Baudot code (later renamed as the 5-bit telex alphabet). The other main system was Continuous Wave (CW) often referred to as Radio-Telegraphy which was used to transmit Morse Code. CW still remains a viable form of radio communication many years after voice transmission was perfected, because simple, transmitters can be used, and the simple on/off keying modulation, its able to penetrate interference. *(sorry, another lesson over)*!

Back at Ganges, the final Morse code and typing exam eventually came and went and I had now reached the dizzy heights of JRO1 (Junior Radio Operator 1st Class) and I had joined a very exclusive club as a TROG (Trained Recruit of Ganges). My Service number was changed from P123... to D123... and the letter 'V' added onto the end. Apparently moving the 'P' for Portsmouth to 'D' Devonport – but this happened to everyone! I had finally made it and I was now ready to pass-out from HMS Ganges to begin the next phase of specialist technical training at HMS Mercury.

4. THE MERCURY EXPERIENCE

HMS Mercury was the Royal Navy College of Communications situated at Leydene close to Petersfield in Hampshire. This was the time for me to 'really' grow up and start behaving myself and trying hard to stop being distracted so easily. We were not kids anymore and were now treated like grown-ups –we were constantly reminded of this. Our introduction and welcome talk from the Chief Trainer started something like "right lads, this is now serious stuff, so you scratch my back and I won't kick you in the teeth".

The Royal Navy is great at nicknames for everything and everyone: A British Army soldier is called a 'Pongo' – based on the saying – 'where the Army goes, the pong goes'. With the Navy's usual powers of wit and sophistication the RAF were referred to as 'crab fats' (or crabs for short) as their blue/grey uniform was allegedly exactly the same colour as the treatment powder for 'crabs' (pubic lice). The RN has unique nicknames for each of its own trades (branch) too, so Electricians = Greenies; Medical Attendants = Scab Lifters; Aircraft Engineers are WAFUs (meaning Wet and Fucking Useless); Photographers = Snaps; Aircraft Handlers = Chock-heads; Writers = Scribes; Stores accountants = Jack Dusty; Seaman = Dab-toes; Divers = Bubble Heads;

Marine Engineers = Stokers; Shipwrights = Chippy; Naval Police (Regulators) = Crushers. I'm sure there's a few more that I've missed.

The Comms branch is split into different groups with different trade badges, depicting the specific specialities: I was listed as a 'G' meaning, General - dealing with radio spectrum sciences, antenna systems, cryptography, radio transmitters and receivers, Morse code and teletype – this trade was known as 'Sparkers'. Ironic really, thinking of the day I failed the 9th week CW exam back in Ganges. Other specialists were T= tactical, dealing with Flags, lights, voice radio and message handling – known as Buntings, and W = Electronic Warfare, dealing with radar tracking and monitoring – known as Gollies. The Golly group allegedly got their nickname as the branch was fairly new, so promotion was quick – said to get a promotion if you managed to collect a number of Gollies from Robinsons jam-jars (although I have heard other versions). So, I held the magical rank of JRO1(G) but referred to by others as a 'baby Sparker'.

The new curriculum was pretty concentrated and included the Navy's new Integrated Communications System (ICS). The ICS is a set of hardware devices that allows communications interfaces as diverse as conventional UHF, VHF, HF and analogue radio-telecommunications including telephony. ICS also has a series of 'Dummy Load' devices used to simulate an electrical load, usually for testing purposes. In radio a dummy antenna is connected to the output of a radio transmitter and electrically simulates an antenna, to allow the transmitter to be adjusted and tested without radiating radio waves. It is important to understand the radio wave (so to calculate half and quarter-wave) so we could design and build wire antennae systems for high frequency services. We also learned about ionospheric propagation: In radio communication, skywave or skip refers to the propagation of radio waves reflected or refracted back toward Earth from the ionosphere, an electrically charged layer of the upper atmosphere. Since it is not limited by the curvature of the Earth, skywave propagation can be used to communicate beyond the horizon, at intercontinental distances. It is mostly used in the HF frequency bands. The final part was the transmitting of military confidential signals around the world, which meant we needed to learn about encryption and Cryptography. These specialist machines are for automatic encryption using a composition of mixed alphabet substitutions performed by means of rotors. An example of such a machine would be the famous German Enigma machine used in WWII. We were trained and tested on a device known as the TSEC/KL7. *This is turning into a technical training lesson again – my apologies – but bringing back memories of fun days.*

This was very intense training but I just loved it and soaked up the knowledge like a sponge. (I guess I must have done because it all seems so fresh in my head, even today). HMS Mercury was very close to my home town of Winchester, so most weekends, I was able to head home to catch-up with the family and to have a few pints in the Wykeham Arms with my old school buddies. Yes, they were still panel beating, car mechanics, welding, painting and decorating, but it was fun to be so close to home. There were many occasions when I would take a few matelot friends home too, and as normal, my Mum would make a big fuss of them all. My new mates would make a fuss of the girls in Winchester too, so we usually found ourselves in the pubs, swinging the lamps and telling sea stories, and swapping addresses (didn't have internet or mobile phones in 70s).

It was always nice to be home BUT - the Mercury Club and NAAFI bar always had a disco of their own on Sunday nights with DJ Steve – so getting back there on time was paramount. My Dad discovered a few short cuts through country lanes, and managed to get me back to camp in just 22minutes. A pretty good record for an old Escort van.

Captain's divisions at Mercury was a big joke, as having learned to march at Ganges with the bugle band or, if we were lucky, we had a visiting band of the Royal Marines. The

Mercury divisions always ended with the march past and salute, but with music played on an old long-playing record which was so scratchy and often jumped too. A few skips and a jump to get into step, but then out of step again as the sound faded before we even reached the end of the path.

One thing we noticed right away, was that our fortnightly pay increased from £3 to £7.50, and again later to £15. Every other payday – so once a month, we would also be handed three 'RN Tobacco Ration Stamps'. We would trade these stamps at the ship's stores for cigarettes or tobacco (3 stamps = 300 plain/Filter ciggies, or 3/4lb Pipe tobacco, or 3/4 lb Cigarette rolling tobacco). Known as 'Blue Liners', these were said to be the worse cigarettes you could ever smoke. The ciggies came in silver foil packs of 100, one for each stamp (coupon). 300 being the monthly maximum whilst ashore. These were made for the Navy by 'Sobrane or British Associated Tobaccos' and they had a blue line down the length of the cigarette with the words H.M. Ships only. Each month that coupon was date-stamped so they couldn't be saved up and carried over. At HMS Mercury we were able to draw our allowance and pay just 50p per 100 pack – so £1.50 for your months' supply of 300 cigarettes. There was a strict allowance on leaving the ship though – so night leave was 25 cigarettes; Long Leave of 7 days or more was 200 cigarettes, no matter what the length of leave. The limit was enforceable by the Crushers on leaving the base, or by the MOD Police on passing through the dockyard gate. Many regulators turned a blind eye but the MOD-Plod did not, but we didn't see much on MOD Plod in this small community at Mercury.

I loved my time at Mercury for many reasons, the training, the relaxed almost family-like atmosphere, the location, proximity to my home town of Winchester and the facilities were fabulous. The Mercury club, the NAAFI shop, the swimming pool, Saturday football, Sunday cricket and much more tranquil than Ganges. Everything was easier and at the slower pace – leaving the base was allowed and easy to do as there is public main road running right through the centre. Even taking the long walk down to the nearest village of Clanfield where there was a collection of pub choices and laundromat heaven! We would often double-up on the washing machines – one for blues - one for whites, then pop into the Rising Sun pub across the road for a beer or two whilst the laundromat did its work. Often, we couldn't remember the walk back to Mercury, and the walk didn't take as long! Sometimes on a Friday afternoon, there would be a liberty bus to Petersfield and/or to Portsmouth, so a Saturday day-trip out would be planned – the latter would usually mean a trip to The Arches Tattoo studio close to the dockyard gates (my very first tattoo was here), and then an evening spent in Southsea, at Joanna's night club. This Southsea night club was sarcastically nicknamed the 'Royal Navy School of Dancing' and famous for its papier mâché tree and carpets that were very much like sticky glue as your shoes stuck when you walked. Joanna's was a huge favourite of many matelots in the 1970s. Unfortunately, it was also a haunt for local Pompey football fans, all dressed in their skinhead regalia and usually, after a few beers or a bad result at Fratton Park, were looking for a fight with a matelot.

Of course, Saturday was also Football day, so whenever the Saints played at home, and if I wasn't on weekend duty, I would sometimes try to get tickets for the game at the Dell. There was a new manager at Saints, Lawrie McMenemy, who was reported to be building a new Saints team of older experienced players like Peter Osgood join Saints from Chelsea and defender Jim Steele from Rangers, to complement some of the juniors, and hoping to get a good run in the first division. With Martin Chivers banging in the goals, this left Saints high enough in the league for them to qualify for the UEFA Cup and I was lucky enough to see a UEFA game at the Dell – sadly we did make a quick exit from the competition – losing to Athletic Bilbao in the first round – but the Dell was a great place to be and the football was getting better under the new manager.

Back at Mercury, the final week of exams was approaching fast, so the class would sit around together and shoot questions at each other, every evening. The Morse and typing classes also continued but the speeds and accuracy counts were very high. We were no longer using typewriters and had upgraded to teleprinters, which made the speed targets a little easier. The difference with the teleprinter was that we need to enter two CRs and one LF instead of manually pushing the bar back after the bell. I passed all subjects with good grades and now we could all relax and wait for our draft chits to come through. Time for fun and frolics.

After just a few weeks finishing up, we were all looking forward to going home for the Christmas break, but didn't know what was to come next. We were all summonsed to the Admin Office for our drafts. Everyone was very excited and had some ideas of their first preference for a ship – I just wanted to wait/see what was available. The PO started listing the warships by name, and for some strange reason, he looked directly at me and said "right Willis, you're first. What do you want?" I immediately shouted HMS Ark Royal please POTs. The room went silent for a moment, then everyone just laughed – at me! "All those Leanders' and you chose Ark Royal – what were you thinking"? I didn't care, as I was delighted that I was going home for Christmas, then joining the most powerful warship in the Royal Navy - the 55,000-ton Aircraft Carrier - HMS Ark Royal. Wow and double-WOW!

5. FIRST WARSHIP – HMS ARK ROYAL

Beaming with excitement, I couldn't wait for Christmas to be over, so I could head off to Plymouth. It was early January 1973 when I took the long train journey down to Devon and walked up the gangway to board the ship. There were several of my Mercury classmates too: Joey Sheppard, Mick Ennis, Lofty Hewitt and Stan O'Connor. We were all quite excited – but nervous too. Once onboard, we met the killick of the mess, and were taken to 5k1 which was our new home (*Remember, deck 5, section K, Starboard side!*)

HMS Ark Royal (R09) was an Audacious-class aircraft carrier and was the last remaining conventional catapult and arrested-landing aircraft carrier. She was the first aircraft carrier to be equipped with angled flight deck at its commissioning. Ark Royal was officially launched in February 1955 by Her Majesty the Queen Mother and was the only non-United States vessel to operate the McDonnell Douglas Phantom at sea. By 1970, Ark Royal had a complement of 39 aircraft comprising 12 Phantom FG fighters, of 892 Naval Air Squadron, 14 Buccaneer of 809 Squadron, 2 Gannet AEW (Airborne Early Warning) of B Flight 849 Squadron, 7 Sea King HAS Mk1 of 824 Squadron and 2 Wessex HAR Mk1 of the Ship's Flight. At last, I had made it – I was now going to serve real sea-time and my boyhood dreams were all starting to come true. I just couldn't wait to get stuck in!

The next nice surprise was pay day, and delighted to see yet another pay rise as my fortnightly rate went up to £26.50. Apparently, this rise was attributed to the fact that, whilst at sea, there is no charge for food and accommodation – as the latter was a poor standard compared to barracks. I couldn't agree more, as 5k1 mess was quite small, yet housed 35 of us, stacked in bunk beds three high. The bathroom offered just two showers and five washbasins – so even more cramped.

As one of the Juniors onboard, we had been warned about practical jokes being played by the older seadogs who ask that you do certain 'silly' tasks. You know the ones, 'go get me a tin of tartan paint' – or 'can you get some white paint for the last post', or a bubble for the spirit level! They say that being warned is being well armed, so when I was told, 'go to the chief buffer and get me a long weight [long wait] I knew what I was up for. "Right mate" I replied and off I went – to the NAAFI shop for some nutty, then off to the main mess for a cuppa, then off up to the flight deck for a walk around and explore. I was exploring the ship for at least an hour before returning to 5k1, and found everyone laughing at how gullible [they thought] I was. One guy even explained the joke to me. They didn't like the idea that I knew of these credulous jokes, and told them of my exploring around the flight deck, normally out-of-bounds to non WAFU trade. The joke was on them this time, but it hasn't stopped me trying them out on others. There was one that (almost) got me though – I was in the MCO repairing the torn pages in the RNCP (RN Communications Publication) ring-binder files, using those sticky linen washers around the holes. We were close to running out of washers, so I asked the Duty Watch killick where I might get more. He suggested that I went to the MCO Lower stationary cupboard and ask. "How many will I get" I asked; the LRO replied "just ask for a hat full of holes". Off I went...

Within just three days onboard, HMS Ark Royal sailed to the Mediterranean for aircraft trials off Gibraltar, with shore visits scheduled for a few days. There were two MCOs (Main Communications Office), Upper and Lower, the latter being occupied by the Buntings message handling teams. I was introduced to the MCO Upper which was the ships telecommunications hub, and I was now going to put into practice all the training I had had over the last 18months. MCO Upper, was on deck-02 so a walk to work from mess to office was akin to climbing the stairs of a 7-storey building.

The MCO was filled with teleprinters, telex tape cutters and readers, and had a number of different 'bays' providing different comms circuits/channels. My first job as a baby Sparker was as 'Recorder' – this is, as the name implies, registering and logging every single message in and out of the ship. Incoming messages were mainly from the Fleet Broadcast operators on a series of teleprinters. These were sorted by different 'urgency' shown on the message itself, where those marked 'immediate' (or above) had a 30minutes turn-around so had to be brought to the attention of the RSOW (Radio Supervisor of the watch – a Petty Officer). Outgoing messages went through a series of different processes – signatory authorisation, urgency, routing, tape-cutting, assigned log/registration number - usually the Date and Time Group (DTG) and then sent by the most appropriate channel. Being the Recorder was a great way to get to know everyone else's job and how the in/out message flow worked. After a few weeks of this, we were moved around and I took over a Fleet Broadcast Operator. Unfortunately, that was the limit of being a 'junior' but as we developed our skills, the job-list got bigger and better as we looked to learn other roles including the UHF/VHF room or the Communications Control Room (CCR) on deck-6. The CCR was a room filled from deck to deckhead with radio receivers and transmitters, and the control equipment required to get signals transmitted from/to the MCO, the operations room, the bridge or any other areas of the ship. At the centre of the CCR was the main Control and Maintenance (C&M) desk. This was usually run by an experienced LRO and was the heartbeat of the whole ships communications systems, so a vital link to keep in touch with the world. Juniors were often given training on how to use the equipment, connecting dummy loads, fine tuning antennae and 'making live' any requests for service. The LRO also ran the Radio-Telephony (RadPhone) connectivity to those who wanted to make radio calls home. An expensive option which I avoided.

Learning my trade in the CCR

I loved being at sea and often used my spare time just sitting and watching the ocean as it rushed by. Between shifts (off watch) I discovered a very quiet place on deck-4, beside the Captain's Launch, where I could sit with my legs hanging over the side of the ship, listening to music on my portable cassette player, and write letters home. Thinking back now, this was a bit silly because had I ever fallen overboard, no-one would ever have heard or seen me go over.

Once through the straights of Gibraltar, the ship entered flying stations and I was able to go the top decks to watch the fighter jets taking off and landing onboard. The Fleet Air Arm (FAA) operates all the Royal Navy's aircraft. A vital element for many of the wide and varied roles undertaken by the Royal Navy, FAA roles range from humanitarian operations, through to securing the seas, fighting terrorism and landing troops onto hostile shores. HMS Ark Royal carried technologically advanced aircraft of that time, and witnessing these noisy fighters was a totally amazing experience.

Finding my way around Ark Royal was fairly easy as most things you needed were around the 'main drag' which was the deck-4: The Post Office, the Dentist, sick bay, NAAFI Shop, the Reg Office and the duty-free cigarette store to name a few. Duty free cigarettes were available once the ship had left the UK 12-mile zone and where I was able to buy Embassy Kings or No6 King size in 200 packs – 10 days' supply for just £2.25!

My first foreign run ashore was in Gibraltar - a British Overseas Territory and headland, on Spain's south coast. It's dominated by the Rock of Gibraltar, a 426m-high limestone ridge. On my first visit ashore, it was strange to see traditional UK red phone boxes, fish-and-chip shops and creaky 1970s seaside hotels: Gibraltar it seemed was just like an old saying I once heard - 'a piece of Portsmouth sliced off and towed 500 miles south'. The Rock overstates its Britishness, a bonus for pub-grub and a British tax-free haven poised strategically at the gateway of Europe and Africa, the Rock played an admirable supporting role during the world wars and has been governed by the British since 1713 - longer than the United States has been American. I went ashore with George and Geoff, two experienced seadogs but we spent most of the day ascending the Rock of Gibraltar by cable car, chasing the famous rock apes (Barbary Macaques) from our food and drinks, and touring the underground tunnels. The tunnels of Gibraltar were constructed by the British Army. It's interesting to learn that Gib has a land area of only 2.6 square miles yet there are about 30+ miles of tunnels, nearly twice the length of its entire road network. The 20th century witnessed the greatest extent of tunnelling when the Rock was turned into a huge underground fortress capable of accommodating 16,000 men along with all the supplies, ammunition and equipment needed to withstand a prolonged siege. The tunnelling finally ceased in 1968 when the British Army's last specialist tunnelling unit was disbanded.

It wasn't too long before George and Geoff introduced me to the John Collins Cocktail — a kind of Gin and Bitter lemon with angostura bitters. After a few of these and a couple of pints, I was dragged back onboard ship having lost the few souvenirs (rabbits) that I had purchased for the family back home. I never did find my camera either - an ongoing 'sea story' and life-lesson of my own and a story that has given me a lot of mileage since.

One of the jobs as a RO whilst the ship was alongside, was to man the ships main telephone exchange. This was an old Strowger electromechanical stepping switch telephone exchange system. A basic system with an electrically operated rotary switch with a single input, and multiple output terminals. Whilst the Greenies looked after the maintenance, our job was to operate the manual PBX, so answer telephone calls into the ship and manually route them to the right destination. This was quite a boring and lonesome task, but later we learned to use this as an advantage to benefit the RO's.

The ship sailed again into the Mediterranean and away towards Malta. Malta is a small island country in central Mediterranean between Sicily and the North African coast.

In 1964, British Parliament passed the 'Malta Independence Act' giving Malta independence from the UK with it becoming the State of Malta, with Queen Elizabeth II as its head of state, and queen. The country became a republic in 1979 when the Royal Navy left the country for the last time bringing the end to a lasting friendship and strategic RN base. I had heard many stories of Malta from my Dad who named the island as 'the land of bells and smells' marking his own view on the strict religious culture and the popularity of a certain street near the harbour.

Ark Royal squeezed into Grand Harbour, Malta

Strait Street runs parallel to Republic Street and in those days was full of bars from one end to the other. When the Fleet was in it was full of sailors spending their wages on wine, women and song. Strait Street was the main meeting place and every matelot knew where it was, as it was one of the liveliest parts of the capital, particularly after dark. The area was Malta's precious economic lifeline in the Valletta street known as Strait Street and unflatteringly dubbed 'The Gut' by British sailors. It is the narrowest street in the parallel patchwork of grid streets that make-up Valletta. I was determined not to get stuck in the same drinking routine as Gibraltar a few weeks earlier, so no JC cocktails, less beer and more culture and sightseeing. I teamed up with a few other guys in search of the sunshine and beaches. Malta has a long and rich history, and this is reflected in the island's cultural attractions. There are also a number of aquatic activities to enjoy on Malta as well as the North Island, Gozo. I almost fell for another practical joke, as I read a message on the mess noticeboard asking for volunteers for the Malta Dog Shoot. "Shooting dogs", I thought, can this be true? Inevitably I was always destined to be found later, heading to 'the street'.

Strait street was filled with bars, restaurants and entertainment halls brimming with sailors, bar maids, musicians and anyone generally out to have a good time.

Ladies of the night hung around every corner, and were part of the entertainment offering in the street. Prostitution played a big part – it was a main attraction for the many drunken sailors, and also a way of making money for the many poverty-stricken individuals and families living in the lower part of Valletta. Of course, as a Junior we were warned to be careful when entering the bars, as you would immediately have a bar-tab opened and a few beers and some other green-coloured drinks on the bill – even though you had no idea. The famous drinks were known as 'sticky greens' – so if a young lady (or old lady come to that) came to sit on your lap, the best thing to do would be to throw her off straight away before your bar-tab was opened without you knowing.

The only way off the ship, and back on after dark, was via a water taxi known as a Dghajsa (pronounced di-so). These were mainly used in the area of the Grand Harbour, to carry passengers. The boat was usually propelled by one man standing, facing forward, and pushing on two oars. The high stem and stern pieces seemed to be mainly ornamental but they are useful in handling the boat and in the boarding and disembarking of drunken passengers. The decorative symbols vary from boat to boat. HMS Ark Royal set sail again and headed back towards Gibraltar and then full steam ahead home to Plymouth. I was to travel again to Malta in the 1990s for a business trip, and clearly it remains a major tourism hot bed in the Mediterranean.

1973 was the year I turned 18 which meant FOUR big changes were coming my way. By far the most exciting was my very first issues of a beer ration card. As the Rum Tot was discontinued a few years prior, each rating was now issued three standard cans of beer per day. The labels I remember included, McEwans Export, Tennants Piper, Tartan Ale or Harp Lager. Interesting choices had to be consumed every day as stockpiling was not allowed, although many people hid some away for 'channel night' celebrations – the night before we got back home. The second thing about 'coming-of-age' was that I was no longer a Junior and was automatically changed to RO3(G). The jobs in the MCO didn't change, nor the daily routines, but the pay did, a little. I was now paid £29/fortnight – I thought I was rich! The third change was the length of time I would serve in the Royal Navy. As a 15-year old I signed to serve for 12 years, but this regulation was changed because at aged 15, we were not considered 'adult' to make that decision. I was offered the opportunity to sign again, but for either 9 years, or 3 years. The latter would mean a drop in pay by 50p/day, but also meant I could leave the service at the age of 21 years. I decided to sign for just 3 years but with an option to make another change again later if I thought differently. Finally, the fourth big change meant that I was no longer a junior so I didn't have to be back onboard ship after a night out, before midnight. This last point meant that I could now go to Plymouths best - 'Club Cascade' (and others) with my shipmates.

Back in Plymouth we had about 4 weeks to prepare for the long summer deployment, and to get some home time with the family. I went to meet up with the old school mates and to tell them of my first sea-stories of my experiences in Gibraltar and Malta. The guys were finishing their trade courses and apprenticeships in panel beating, mechanics, welding, butchery, as well as painting and decorating, but they were all very interested in my life as a matelot and to hear my tales of the sea – you know, the one that always starts "when I was in….

On return to Guzz (the matelot name for Plymouth) I was sent over to the Devonport Signals Training Centre (STC) to start my training on ICS1 equipment and to prepare for my RO2(G). A Second-Class Radio Operator was the natural exam-based promotion so I had to work hard, and after a few weeks training I was tested and passed. According to my 'Communications Ratings History Sheet' the Signal Communications Officer (SCO) Lt. George Evatt wrote *"Willis is competent for RO2 as a Fleet Broadcast Operator, on a CW circuit, as a tape perforator and as an Admin on a voice circuit"*. I was very pleased to see this comment, and to be promoted as it meant another [small] pay-rise which lifted me over the £30/fortnight rate and I was given a one-star trade badge in recognition.

During our time in Guzz, I was introduced to Union Street – the 'go-to' place in town for a good night out. A mile-long street lined with many pubs and clubs, each with a different theme and a different atmosphere. The main haunts were The Two Trees, the London Bar, German Beer Keller, Antelope, Diamond Lil's, The Pussycat, Ace of Clubs and many more. A good night out usually ended with a taxi ride back to the dockyard and a fish supper to finish off back onboard. Union street also hosted the tattoo artist known as Doc Price. A small studio where the walls inside are adorned with colourful designs. Of course, I had to go see the Doc on a few occasions, just to have the 'tatts' topped up, for that 'real sailor' look.

Back on the telephone PBX duty, we would sit and take calls from dockyard workers, officers, Captain enquiries and of course, the lonely girls in Plymouth looking for 'Smudge Smith' the matelot they met the night before, or anyone else who might talk to them. One evening I took a call from a local girl looking to make arrangements to go on a blind date with someone. We suggested that we would meet the following evening outside the main cinema in Plymouth town, and she would bring a friend. The next evening, Joey and I headed off to the cinema and whilst waiting outside, we were approached by these two girls – and if I'm honest, they were not the prettiest girls I've met before. They approached and asked if I was Alan from Ark Royal. I quickly replied, "sorry, no love – I'm George and we're from HMS Fearless" and made a quick exit. When I explained this to the guys back in 5k1, it was suggested that I should have at least taken a picture for the mess 'gronk board'. The GB is a strange phenomenon that would be completely un-PC in these days, but is a messdeck noticeboard where photos of ugly girls that you've 'trapped' (pulled) or ex-girlfriends would be posted. Some messes had quality gronk boards. The PBX duty was always time to make a joke and try to catch-out your mess-mates. If you were asked for someone who wasn't available on their usual/published extension number, the operator had the ability to pipe the whole ship over the Tannoy system. Often you might hear pipes for "MEM Brain" – I was caught out by "RO Tate". There are many others like this, so you had to be on your guard.

At this time, we witnessed the very untimely death of our Mess Killick Martin 'Mo' Morrissey who was involved in a road traffic accident. He was a pillion passenger on a motorcycle ridden by VinceC, an RO2 also from 5k1 mess. Mo was killed instantly and Vince ended up having both knees badly damaged. The Fleet Chief RS, Mr. Shuker, arranged a mini-bus to get some of the guys to Mo's funeral. Shortly following the burial, there was a very strange 'auction of kit'; The selling of the contents of the dead man's locker is a Navy traditional final ritual commemorating the death of a sailor aboard ship. After the burial, the men would all muster on deck and then auction off each item with the intent of sending the money raised to the dead man's family. The practice was so common that muster books were even printed, and if you purchased something, the money was deducted directly from pay, and all proceeds went towards 'Dead Man's Clothes Fund'. We mustered in one of the lower hangers onboard, and the bidding started. I'd never heard of this practice before and it was very strange to see my shipmates bidding to buy the kit, then offering it back into the auction. This tradition also became an effective way to distribute used goods among the crew and also connected the sailor at sea to his family on land. Among us sailors, our late shipmate's possessions could also serve as a sentimental reminder. I'm not sure how much was raised for the family, but this was a really nice way to give a brilliant send-off to Mo. Our new Killick of the mess was a Manchester lad Maurice 'Mo' O'C.

6. USA AND BEYOND

In May 73 HMS Ark Royal was now ready to set sail on a long deployment to join up with the Americans for some NATO war games on exercise in the north Atlantic, and then some down-time in the Caribbean and USA. Exercises at sea meant long watchkeeping stints, NBCD training, Ships emergency drills (floods, fires, casualties) and ships black-out. 'Darken ship' meant that every light had to be covered up, or switched off and side-scuttles (also known as 'port holes' if you're non-maritime) had to be closed and covered. Often, the ship would also go into radio silence too, but that didn't mean time for a sleep for us Radio Operators, as the incoming messages kept flooding in via the Fleet Broadcast. Watch-keeping (or shift working) was difficult at first, but over time it just became second nature.

0800 – 12:00: Forenoon Watch
1200 – 1600: Afternoon Watch
1600 – 2000: Double Dog Watch (usually two dog watches 1600-1800 and 1800-2000)
2000 – 0200: Long First (sometimes a middle watch from 2200-0200)
0200 – 0800: Long Morning

In extreme war-games, we would often operate 6-hours on and 6-hours off – 24x7 for the duration, but in-between these times, we still had to clean, eat and sleep – or no sleep if there was an NBC attack. Great memories of good times.

Eventually, we finished the NATO exercises and were due to take some down-time. It was announced that a few days in St Thomas, the US Virgin Island would provide a small mini-break after such an intense period of training and hard work, so we were looking forward to a few days on the beach in the sunshine.

Saint Thomas is one of the Virgin Islands in the Caribbean Sea and, together with Saint John, and Saint Croix, form a county and constituent district of the United States Virgin Islands (USVI), an unincorporated territory of the United States. Located on the island is the territorial capital and port of Charlotte Amalie. St. Thomas is the most cosmopolitan of all USVI, yet it still retains the distinctive atmosphere of a Caribbean paradise. There is plenty of duty-free shopping, spectacular diving and world-class picture-perfect beaches. It was great to get ashore, laze on the beach, have a few beers and enjoy the nightlife. But time was short and the Ark Royal had 2,500 personnel to rotate for some R&R before we headed off to sea again for more exercises, and witnessing the Phantom and Buccaneers fighter jets let-loose their fierce armament cannons and taking pot shots at a splash target being towed by the Ark Royal.

Buccaneer of 809 Naval Air Squadron,

The Ark Royal's complement of Phantom fighters could hit a top speed of over Mach 2.2 and can carry more than 18,000 pounds (8,400 kg) of weapons on nine external hardpoints, including air-to-air missiles, air-to-ground missiles, and various bombs. The Buccaneer provided the Royal Navy's ability to attack enemy ships by approaching at high speed and low altitudes below the ship's radar horizon. The Buccaneer could carry nuclear weapons if required, or conventional weapons. It was later intended to carry short-range anti-shipping missiles to improve its survivability against more modern ship-based anti-aircraft weapons. Both the Phantom and Buccaneer, like other interceptors of its time, were deadly in their approach and boy, these Royal Navy pilots were very good at their job and for us it was fascinating to be able to watch the action from the upper decks. Just watching them prepare for take-off from the flight deck was simply spectacular. Ark Royal launched the aircraft via two steam powered catapults, so powerful they were capable of launching aircraft weighing up to 13½ tons. Landing was more difficult as this was based on a new 'mirror landing system' and arrestor cables, so as the plane hit the flight deck, it also dropped a 'hook' which caught on the cables – therefore catching the plane. The G-Force on take-off and landing must have been an awful experience, but these innovations allowed aircraft to land and take off from the carrier at the same time.

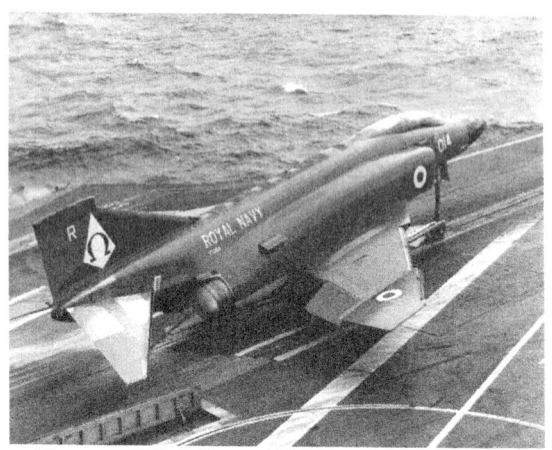

Phantom FG fighter of 892 Naval Air Squadron

War games finally ended and we were heading for the

British Virgin island of Virgin Gorda for another mini-break and to fly the Union Jack at a British Virgin Island. This was a stop to let our hair down and celebrate the end of three weeks of very hard work, and to have some fun with a beach Banyan. The Ark was too big to go alongside, so we anchored off the coast and a flotilla of liberty boats were launched to take us to a remote beach, well away from the tourists. The boats were filled with 'Jack' in his beachwear tee shirts, shorts and flip—flops, speedos wrapped in a towel and a crate of beer over the shoulder. It was party time!

Back onboard, we now had some serious 'Union Jack Flying' business to do and to get the ship looking clean, tidy and painted ready for a series of visits to US Navy bases and some high-visibility stops on the USA mainland. First stop was at Roosevelt Roads US Naval Station – a large United States Navy base in the town of Ceiba on the Caribbean island of Puerto Rico. This was a refuelling and store replenishment stop for the ship, and yet another good run ashore for the crew. 'Roosy' is just a short taxi ride from the small town of San Juan which became a popular spot for a night out with one particular night club taking most of the business – the Black Angus Club was the trendy place to be, with cheap beer, live music and plenty of on-stage strippers, and even live sex. The Commonwealth of Puerto Rico is an archipelago among the Greater Antilles including Cuba, Hispaniola, Jamaica, and the Cayman Islands. Six island states share the region of the Greater Antilles in total with a landscape of mountains, waterfalls and the popular El Yunque tropical rainforest. Roosevelt Roads military base has its own fantastic beach area exclusive for the Navy and families and it was great to chill in the sunshine and enjoy a beer or two.

Fully laden with stores, fuel and crew, the next stop was the island of Barbados. This place has a fascinating history, first claimed by the Spanish Crown and appeared in a Spanish map in 1511. The Portuguese then took the island but later abandoned it. An English ship, the Olive Blossom, arrived in Barbados in 1625 and took possession of it in the name of King James I. In 1627, the first permanent settlers arrived from England, and it became English and later an independent British Commonwealth nation. Bridgetown was our landing place and the local town and where a number of organised outings were arranged by the ship.

Most of us simply took a taxi into Bridgetown and the beaches; one of the best beaches we found was Browne's beach, close to a group of the bigger posh hotels. We also did a brief tour of the Mount Gay rum distillery, which was a must for some of the older guys remembering the old days of the Tot. We then asked the taxi driver to take us to a traditional 'local' bar – somewhere there was no giant hotels or commercialism. After a short drive, we found ourselves in a small township and a bar owned by Mrs Roach who greeted us like we were family, and she moved a crate of beer onto our table as we all tucked in and listened to the local folklore. She loved having us around and offered us plenty of snacks including the famous flying-fish sandwich. Flying fish were often very visible when we were at sea, but I'd never thought of eating one. This was a local delicacy which we all enjoyed.

Back in the taxi, the next stop was a visit the famous Nelson street area, filled with bars, live music and red-lights. As we entered the New York bar, we were greeted by a group of young girls leading us towards the bar and ordered drinks on our behalf, and one for themselves. They only had one plan and a few British sailors were all they needed to get the party rolling. As the girls and matelots started to get themselves into pairs, one girl came over to me and started to massage my thigh. "Do you want to fu*k me" she said. Well, how do you decline an offer like that (rhetorical question). Whilst I mused over my answer, I glanced upstairs to the landing where there was a queue of matelots, each holding a plastic bucket. There were a number of different coloured buckets. I learned that each colour was connected to one of the girls and the sailors were waiting for a bedroom to become available. The bucket was for the girls to squat over and wash themselves before entertaining the next guy. My decision was made, "No thanks" I said. Some may have heard the phrase 'sloppy seconds', well in this case you may have had sloppy thirds, fourths or even tenths – who knew!

HMS Ark Royal, the flagship of the UK fleet was now looking great – a new paint job, gleaming and shining from every corner. We were sailing to the Eastern seaboard of the United States, with Fort Lauderdale Florida as our destination. Fort Lauderdale is a city on Florida's southeastern coast, known for its beaches and boating canals. The main drag is a promenade of upscale hotels, outdoor restaurants, bars, boutiques and luxury goods shops. Once again, the ships office had scheduled some organised tours and we were destined to stay in Fort Lauderdale for at least 14 days.

Our shifts were all arranged so everyone could maximise their runs ashore. I teamed up with Joey and a few others and we headed for our first day trip to Walt Disney World, a 3-hour Greyhound bus ride away, so up and away early and a fantastic day all round. Initially, we thought this was going to be a bit like 'a family day out – but without the family', but we were excited about seeing this famous place. Apart from there being a strict no-alcohol policy, it was one of the best days, and one where we spent far too much money and brought home all the souvenirs we could carry.

The next day I was on duty on the ships Telephone Exchange but it wasn't going to be an easy shift. The Ships office had set-up a couple of plans to invite the locals onto the ship, and to provide the opportunity to take sailors home with them – a so-called 'dial a sailor' system. We were given strict instruction to route any incoming calls from locals to the Captains Office team who would allocate families to British sailors. It was early into the shift when the exchange became flooded with calls and it wasn't long before the call queue was building up too. We were able to sneak a few calls through to the Comms team messdeck directly, so we could arrange our own 'Grippo' – a Grippo is a person(s) who would take you out, feed you, buy you beer and generally entertain you for the day. Some of the guys had great experiences. Whilst I was on duty, I received a call from a lady who wanted to invite a couple of British sailors to her home. Instead of pushing the call through, I took all her details and arranged to meet her at the gangplank the next day. She told us she would be wearing a red dress and be accompanied by her daughter, and we should bring our swimwear – that's all we would need. Well, what an invitation to get very excited about! Three/four of us got ready and met this lady. It turned out that her daughter was only 7 and she was taking us to her home in the Everglades to meet the rest of her family, including her husband. Initially disappointing, but the day turned out to be just fabulous. Her husband worked in the Port of Miami Authority and he kept us busy with his tales of living and working by the Everglades, and how the odd alligator would wonder across the greens at the local golf course. There was some [beer] talk of taking us to the Alligator farm to see a show, or an airboat rides across the glades – but neither of these happened. Meanwhile, we had a poolside barbeque and had the opportunity to make home-made burgers, had plenty of beer and returned safely to the ship that evening.

The next day we were completely knackered, so Joey and I went only as far away as Fort Lauderdale beach. This is a great beach with probably many miles of golden sand, and we were told one that has a superior quality beach (and less drugs and violence) than the famous Miami, just a few miles down the coast. We hired a few mini-surf boards and spent almost the whole day riding waves, laying in the gorgeous sunshine, eating local burgers and drinking the local beer, Pabst Blue Ribbon which was pretty poor but the cheapest on the beachside store. This day of 'just chilling' proved to be a total remedy for my ADD simply because we had nothing else to think about, just looking out for each other.

Day 11 and it was my turn to stay onboard again, but instead of working the PBX, I had to escort locals on a tour of the warship. It was a scorching hot day, the queue to get onboard was huge, and my job was to stand on the flight deck and dip the ensign whenever a ship came/went into the harbour. This was strange job for me as I had no bunting training, so I just dipped the ensign whenever another ship did it first. Most of the day was spent posing for photographs with tourists, beside the ensign. I didn't mind that job, but wearing only half-blues, the back of my neck had sun-burned quite badly, so I was glad when the day ended of me, but another day of grippo tours for the others.

My final day in Florida was spent at the John F. Kennedy Space Centre located in Merritt Island, Florida. This is one of ten NASA field centres and is the second launch position after Cape Canaveral – which had to be moved because of the large size of the Apollo Saturn launch module. I remember this when I was a young boy, watching the launch of the Apollo missions, and now I could see the actual returned Apollo-11 capsule that Armstrong, Aldrin and Collins dropped back to earth in. There was also a superb replica of the 'Eagle' lunar landing module (of course the original is still on the moon somewhere). This was a serious and educational day out, again without too much beer.

On return to the ship, we were preparing to sail again, the normal routine is for the killick (or PO) of every mess to report the Reg Office to ensure everyone is onboard. We discovered that two of our guys from 5k1 mess had not made it back. In fact, it was announced that Keith and Tom had left the ship on day-1 and had been AWOL for the entire 14 days. The US authorities were alerted and the ship was set ready however, at the eleventh hour, the door opened and in marched the guys. It seems that they got Grippo'd by two young ladies and they spent the whole time onshore, with them.

The queue of visitors waiting to board

They both looked totally knackered (or hungover) and were suffering from serious sunburn – Keith had big sunburn blister on his legs from apparently "getting totally pissed and fell asleep in the sun". From the many stories that followed, they had a brilliant time, but started to regret it when given 14days No9s and stopped shore leave at the next destination – Mayport US Navy Base, Jacksonville Florida.

Back at sea again, we had about 14 days – which is an ideal time to place a formal request form to 'Discontinue Shaving' in an attempt to grow a full beard. Whilst the RAF and Army have rules permitting a moustache only, the Royal Navy tradition is a full set, or nothing – but had to be requested formally to the Master at Arms. At the end of the 14 days trial, we were forced to stand in a line whilst the officer of the day and the Master walked the line doing beard inspection. I was listening to the calls of 'OK' or 'shave-off' as they got closer to me. At my turn, the Master stopped –

glared at me and started laughing – shouting "that looks like a fucking chin strap lad – get it shaved off now". That was my one and only request to discontinue shaving.

One of the many fascinating things about the ships and her crew, was the merry band of Chinese laundrymen onboard. The firm K.P. Lau were resident Chinese nationals who run the laundry, the cobbler shop and tailors and did a fabulous job. Imagine 2,500 serving matelots onboard, so that's a lot of sailors requiring laundry services. All you had to do was place all your washing into a pillow slip, and launch it down a hole in a small hatchway. Even though you might be new to the ship, the same rules applied. The very next day, you could go to the hatchway and quote your laundry number (or explain you're a new guy and a number would be allocated) and your washing was done. Washed, dried, ironed or pressed, ready to wear. My laundry number was 6586 (or 'si-fi-ay-si' when asked) – I often remember insignificant nonsense. When travelling to the US and Caribbean in the summer months, the rig of the day was usually shorts and sandals, although the RN issued sandals were not always comfortable, but K.P. Lau's team of cobblers would hand-make a pair for you at a reasonable cost. They were a very versatile bunch.

Days at sea were often fun, even when the ships PT department decided to arrange deck hockey competitions, or general 'Potted Sports' on the flight deck. We would form into messdeck teams and set out our plans on how to win everything. Competitors and spectators were out in force and it was obvious from the start that the PTIs had created several tough circuit training sessions and other grueling and tireless events for the games. I must add that I can't recall one single event that 5k1 actually won, but it's a great day of fun in the sunshine and a chance to network with shipmates you've never met before.

Naval Station Mayport is a major United States Navy base in Jacksonville, Florida. The port contains a deep harbour that can accommodate aircraft carrier-size vessels. On arrival, we were to be docked opposite the newest US Aircraft Carrier, the USS John F Kennedy. JFK was the only ship of her class and the last conventionally powered carrier built for the United States Navy. The ship was named after the 35th President of the United States, John F. Kennedy, and was nicknamed "Big John". Kennedy was so big; she threw quite a shadow over the Ark Royal. The two ships had agreed a 'sailor exchange' program which was a day-to-day exercise where I volunteered to spend a day onboard JFK, with a US matelot coming the other way. Eventually I managed to get onboard and was taken to the 'Shack' – a mad place, constant music playing, and guys just hanging around drinking coffee, and in a strange way, making our MCO seem a tad dreary. I settled down to meet some of the American crew who spent most of their time taking the piss by mimicking my English accent, albeit badly – then injecting a few stereotypical names likes 'limey'. They asked what my job was onboard Ark Royal, but couldn't understand why I could multi-task as tape perf, or CW, or voice, or managing a RATT channel, etc. when they were specialist in one task only. One guy 'Chuck', asked if I knew Morse code, and then asked if I did send or receive. He was blown away when I suggested I could do both as the yanks have senders and receivers. JFK was massive and seem so unorganised, not like Ark Royal. We didn't go for lunch – we went to chow-down; we didn't have biscuits (or even cookies) – we had huckdummy; and we didn't have corned beef (or corned dog as we know it) – we had salt horse; and when the ice cream machine broke down – the messdeck almost went into rebellion. An interesting day out, but I think I preferred the British versions the best, and I was glad to be back in 5k1, my own safe place.

This was only to be a short visit whilst Ark Royal attempted repairs to one of the main engines. It required a lot of effort from the ship's crew, and civilian dockyard engineers to keep her serviceable between periods back in Guzz. History tells us that the build program of Ark Royal started in 1942 but was then paused at the end of the World War 2. She had been poorly preserved during this period from 1945 to her official launch by HM The Queen Mother in 1955, and much of its machinery was obsolete by the time the build was completed, including its outdated DC electrical systems, later upgraded to some more modern AC systems, resulting in a ship which experienced regular defects and mechanical failure. Breakdowns and equipment failures were often expensive.

The local township Jacksonville Florida was a nice place to visit and had a good selection of bars and clubs, although the best bars, cheapest beer and best quality food, was in the Navy base's very own PX Clubs: PX is the US equivalent of the British NAAFI who operate shops and bars. The PX (now called the Navy Exchange) offers goods and amenities to active servicemen and women, retirees, and certain civvies who work on military bases in the United States, overseas and aboard Navy ships – and of course open to foreign visiting Navy's too.

Next stop, the US Navy base in Norfolk Virginia: Naval Station Norfolk is just massive! This is the headquarters and home port of the US Navy's Atlantic Fleet where the installation occupies 11 miles of pier and wharf space. We just had a few days alongside for Ark Royal to pick up stores and fuel ready for the trip back to Blighty. We did get time to go ashore, but the usual attractions were the bars and clubs in the local township. This was our chance to say goodbye to America and some of the US matelots we had met up with. I remember four of us passing a very loud bar

– Rock music blaring out thru outside speakers. This noise led us into a bar where we ordered four beers. The bar tender suggested we might like a pitcher of beer, with four glasses – but we all looked at each other, nodded and agreed – "No, four pitchers please barman". We ended the night sitting in the middle of the dance floor doing air-guitar to some Black Sabbath track. Eventually, we were asked to leave by the RNP Regulators – but they allowed us to find our own way back to the ship.

Hungover the next day, the ship sailed early on our passage back across the north Atlantic to the UK, but we were not going straight home, as we had a call into Rosyth in Scotland as the Naval Air Squadrons headed back to RAF Leuchars or RAF Lossiemouth. The UK Submarine base in Rosyth was another run ashore that were just were not prepared for – Submariners certainly know how to have all the fun.

7. BACK HOME TO DEAR GUZZ

The grand old lady, HMS Ark Royal was back home in Guzz and about to start a prolonged period in dry dock refit, again. Many of the ships company left, and the rest of us were moved into HMS Drake, the RN Barracks associated with Plymouth dockyard. The dockyard maintenance program started and we were all assigned task for the coming months. Every day we would walk from RNB through the dockyard to Ark Royal to remove, clean and/or replace/rebuild the wire antennae from the upper decks. As a former Ganges mast manner and an assumed 'head for heights', I was given the task of climbing the mast and cleaning.

After just two weeks I was asked to report to the Devonport STC (signals training centre) so I could start my training for the Radio Operator 1st Class examination. Excited about the prospect, I was in a classroom with other Arkers, some were taking part in the 'NATO Naval Communications Competition 1974'. This was very impressive to watch (and hear) but the high-speed Morse code was by far too fast for me to comprehend. Fellow 5k1 lads Colin and George led the campaign for Morse Transmission and Reception, whilst Bunting Mick-L and Hanksey, were leading the flashing light challenge. The crew went across to Bergen in Norway to represent the UK and the report that followed read that our UK team were placed third overall having won two first prizes.

Meanwhile, I was being taken through the RO1(G) curriculum by LRO Mo and RS 'Ron' who were also going to lead the exam on behalf of the SCO (Signals Communications Officer). This meant two weeks of hard study, going over and over the RCE (radio communications equipment) syllabus for HF and VHF services, but the extra effort was well worth it. I was delighted to pass the exam to reach the dizzy heights of RO1(G) and to gain the 2nd star on my trade badge in recognition. Lofty, Mick, Stanley, Joey and I had now all reached the grade and were ready to get back to work.

Unfortunately, this was going to be a long refit so other tasks were being dished out: I was allocated to attend a training course in 'Ship Husbandry' at HMS Daedalus at Lee-on-Solent near Portsmouth. LRO 'Mac' McKeever led a small band of Ark Royal Sparkers to learn how to clean and paint a ship. Not the most exhilarating course, but one that needed to be done if we were to get 5k1 mess back to looking great again. On return to Guzz, Mac decided that the old colour of 'battleship grey' was just too demoralising for a messdeck, so he took it upon himself to have the mess furniture painted light blue. I'm still not sure why he chose that, but 5k1 became the only junior messdeck onboard to have non-standard colours. I was sent to the bathroom at 5L1 to complete the repainting transformation down there too, but this ended badly as no-one had taught me that I needed to take precautions whilst working in an enclosed space with the Nitromors paint stripper, and spent three days in the sick bay with bad chest pains and heavy coughing after inhaling the fumes. Someone else must have finished the bathroom.

A further task for the ships company, was to provide a crew for a small RN Auxiliary vessel RNXS Loyal Chancellor, pennant A1770. This was a small boat used for Ark's Junior Officer training (Command, Navigation, and sea training) and crewed by Arkers. I was appointed as duty RO and the boat did Guzz to Jersey every Monday; Jersey back to Guzz every Friday then the weekend off. One of my jobs was the naughty exchange of the blue ensign to a white ensign as soon as we had left Guzz, and then swap it back once we returned. I had so much fun onboard, and also met up with a shop assistant, Maria, in a Jersey pub one evening. On return to Guzz after the first week, I managed to persuade Ron to let me go back to see Maria again the following week. He agreed, and so I spent every week for about 2 months onboard on weekdays, then home back to Winchester at the weekends - a great time.

One weekend Joey and I decided to take a break, so we travelled down to Newquay on the north coast of Cornwall. It was a glorious summer and the weekend might provide us with something different – Newquay is known for sandy beaches, where waves from the Atlantic Ocean create strong surf - so maybe some surf action, or we might bump into some female holiday makers – or both if we were lucky. What we didn't plan for was the dates we chose was a bank holiday weekend and we just couldn't find any accommodation as everything was booked solid. A few beers into the weekend and still no B&B or hotel available, we crashed in a bus shelter for the night. It was cold and uncomfortable, but at least we were up early on Saturday to continue our search for a B&B. After a full english in a local café we eventually we found somewhere, paid the money and went to the room, and both fell asleep for the rest of the day, waking around 8pm that evening. A weekend and lots of money simply wasted!

Back in RNB Drake, the daily trudge became a little boring after a while, so we were looking at ways to make a difference. The Drake Club was OK, but entertainment was only at the weekends – the NAAFI bar of course, was a cheap evening out and usually a Saturday night disco, or live band would come along. One evening we saw the 'Bonzo Dog Doo-Dah Band' – who remembers them? When Christmas came, the NAAFI Club party was being organised and a new young Scottish band was invited to come along to provide the entertainment. It turned out to be 'The Bay

City Rollers' (who?) apparently they had just launched a single record deal and were on the way up. Little did we know just how much! Local girls were allowed into the club during the evenings, and one-night Joey and I met up with Angie and Sian. We started dating and meeting the girls outside the barracks each evening. The girls lived close to RNB, just across the railway in Keyham so walking them both home after dark wasn't too much of a burden. These girls introduced us to the local Scrumpy bar – known as The Luggers Inn near the Torpoint Ferry terminal. Angie's Dad was a member of the Keyham Labour Club – bring on the entertainment every weekend, and cheap beer at the bar. We went along a few times but my relationship with Angie took a dive. I believe that Joey and Sian continued their relationship, and even got married at some point.

Ark Royal's refit seemed to go on forever; eventually we started getting excited when she came out of dry-dock and back alongside, even though we were not yet allowed to move back onboard to 5k1. One evening at dinner, I saw someone I recognised. This was a lad from my home town of Winchester, named Terry. It seemed that he was also serving on Ark Royal as a Marine Engineer (Stoker) and had been onboard for a while. Normally on the smaller ships, you get to know everyone onboard, but Ark Royal has over 2,500 crew so bumping into everyone, every day was impossible. Terry was slightly older than me so a different year-group at school, and therefore, a different circle of friends, although I knew most of the group. Terry offered me a lift home at the weekend, in return for a donation for petrol, so of course I was buzzing that a cheap trip home would be up for grabs. On Friday afternoon, we met up and drove off in his maroon-coloured Ford Anglia back to Winchester. I learned since, that Tel didn't have a full driving licence and had no car insurance – but I had no cares back then, and this turned out to be a regular occurrence, and a much cheaper way for me see friends and family, albeit with a few risks attached.

During one of many visits back home, I decided to repay some of Noreen's persistence, and go on a date with her.

We went to a steak house in Winchester Broadway where she wanted to explore the possibility of us having a relationship. We started seeing each other on a regular basis, but one day she introduced me to her new baby daughter. I was a little surprised by this time-bomb, but it didn't deter us from seeing each other and actually, I started to enjoy seeing Noreen and her baby. However, after a few get-togethers, Noreen broke the news to me that she had decided to try and rebuild her relationship with the baby's father, and our alliance was over. This was of course, the correct choice for them both, but it didn't stop me feeling upset and a little annoyed. The best thing for me was to return to my safe place as soon as possible- back onboard HMS Ark Royal.

Back in Guzz, more new kit introductions came as we were provided with windproof jackets (referred to as 'Windy-burbs' – Jack's take on windproof Burberry) and a beret. The Windy-burbs has been issued to the dabtoes (seaman branch) for a long time, but not a general issue unless you work on the upper decks. I think the Buntings might have these already. I wasn't over-keen on the beret at first, with it being a little army-esque, but it proved better than losing your traditional white cap every time the wind blew. We would often see piles of caps in the bottom of the dry docks as you walked by. Another change, was that we could now draw special work boots from the stores for use whilst at sea. Work boots in the Royal Navy have long been called 'steaming bats' or just 'bats'. One might struggle to find the exact origin of this name, but like much Jackspeak it has been passed down through generations. The dabtoes, stokers and chefs have had bats for a long time, but these had not always been available to Sparkers (unless you had a Jack Dusty contact). I managed to get an old beaten-up pair from my Stoker mate Terry, which allowed me to take them to the Jack Dusty and request an exchange for a new pair. Of course, everyone's boots look the same, so finding a way to 'label' your own was sometimes difficult. I just cut into the leather upper with the letter 'W' to identify my own. Steaming Bats are a very particular type of footwear with a steel toe-cap for safety and a non-slip sole for use on wet decks, or in a galley. These became very popular as they were much more comfortable than the original issued shoes or boots, and could be polished up to make a passable set of parade boots as well.

Eventually, HMS Ark Royal was fit and ready to go back to sea; we all moved back onboard, and a few new Sparkers joined us to fill the gaps. We welcomed onboard Jeremy, Dennis, Weeks, Horace and a few others, who had all spent time serving in ComCen Northwood, in North London, so the first sea-time for these new lads. At some point here, the Comms Branch hierarchical seniority system changed and these new guys were introduced as RO1s but they only had the one-star trade badges which traditionally was RO2. I had spent many months of training to reach the rank of RO1 with the two-star badge, but this was how it was. A change I had to reluctantly accept!

After sea trails and testing, the ship was ready to set sail again to the Mediterranean, with scheduled stops in Gibraltar and Malta. During one watch, I saw a signal coming in suggesting that volunteers were needed to spend three months at a local Careers Office. I immediately sent in a Request Form Application to be assigned to Southampton, and was accepted. Lofty did the same, and spent three months at Newcastle-Under-Lyme, his local office.

Heading back home to Southampton for this RN Careers Office loan, wasn't a dream job but it did get me into different ideas and views, and the ability to learn interviewing and recruiting, and presentation skills. Yes, I would miss out on another trip to Gib and Malta, but so what. Being home was far more important to me at that time. I had worked out how much money I'd get paid (in advance) which would include additional funds for food and accommodation whilst at home, and the cost of getting from Winchester to Southampton every day. Luckily, my Dad was working on a long-term construction project in Rownhams (close to the town) and so he would drop me each morning, and I would catch the 47 bus back home each evening. Daily tasks included answering the phone; posting Navy News and attending to walk-in queries. The only problem was that I had to wear No1 Uniform (Gold badges) every day, so it became a little tedious, and the wear and tear on the bestie kit was to prove expensive. The Recruiters were all classed as NRPS (Non-Regular Permanent Staff) all ex-regulars who had taken this option to 'retire in uniform' and still get paid the going rate/rank. They were all CPOs and a RM Warrant Officer, and one Lieutenant. A friendly bunch who would go to the pub next door, every lunchtime, for their tot of Navy rum – a routine I got far too familiar with. Being home allowed me to hook-up with Sue, an old girlfriend from my school days and so we embarked on a romance that was only to last a few months as she couldn't handle the time apart whilst I was back onboard Ark Royal and away at sea. During this time, I got the opportunity to see more of the super Saints at the Dell, spending time with my old school mates, and to spend one more Christmas with my family - a good time all round.

8. BACK AT SEA...

It was January 1975. Whilst Southampton was great, I was also pleased to be back in dear old Guzz and onboard the Ark although my time away meant a few changes were made in 5k1 that I wasn't aware of. My old bunk was allocated to someone else during my absence, so I was moved. It turned out to be better as I was now away from the mess square, the TV and the noise. But on the negative, my personal locker space had been invaded and some of my kit had been placed into storage, but not in a nice way – it was just thrown into a box and stowed in a cupboard. I was a little angered by this, but eventually I found most things, although having to re-purchase a new AGR, anti-flash kit, some new white fronts and some bedding. It was an expensive re-joining exercise, but soon I settled down for the next deployment. A couple of new faces had been drafted in, two new Scots - a new killick 'Mac' McK, and RO1 Willy Mac, and an old seadog 'Banjo' who became a great character around the mess with his sea-stories of the old times and another guitar player to join up with Fred, who both shared the new bunk-space. One thing I did miss-out on, was being part of an official Comms Department photograph, taken on the flight deck during their time in Malta. Ark Royal was about to set sail for another run to the United States and the Caribbean, so a second chance to see the Virgin Islands, Barbados and Disney, and catch-up on the things I missed last time out.

Communications Team Sailing Party

No sooner had we sailed out of Guzz, we picked up our usual Soviet shadow. It was not uncommon during the Cold War for Soviet ships to keep close company with ships of the Royal Navy which are engaged on training and exercises. Ark Royal was always of great interest to the Russians and so our little Ruski spy-ship was following again. Back in 1970 (*well before my time onboard*) Ark Royal together with her escorts and some RAF fighters was taking part in a NATO exercise in the Mediterranean. Ark Royal was in international open waters between Malta and Crete and was engaged in night flying exercises. She had begun launching her aircraft and was displaying the appropriate internationally recognised lights which showed that she could not easily manoeuvre. After the launch of the first aircraft a Soviet Kotlin class destroyer approached Ark Royal on a collision course from the starboard bow. Ark Royal took avoiding actions and put her engines at full astern but she was unable to miss the Soviet vessel, whose port quarter struck Ark Royal's port bow. Ark immediately stopped her night flying exercise so that she and her accompanying escort frigate, HMS Yarmouth, could undertake, with Russian vessels, a search for Russian crew members who were understood to be in the water. Although some were picked up, regretfully two are still believed to be missing. Only minor damage was suffered by the Ark Royal and she had no casualties.

A spy ship usually stays in international waters (or at least outside territorial waters), so as to not violate territorial borders. From there, it will use its electronic surveillance equipment to monitor sea and air radio traffic, radar frequencies and also to try to intercept and decrypt coded radio or phone communications. This is mostly done via passive means such as radio receivers or passive sonar. Sometimes however, active measures such as radar or sonar may also be used to detect the movement of aircraft, missiles and/or ships. Our little Russian friend was now following, which meant extra care on radio transmissions and the dumping of gash (rubbish). Back in the 70s it was common practice to dump the ships gash into the sea – and the spy ship would often be seen picking up the gash bags, obviously looking for interesting information, so it was important not to mix confidential waste with general gash. Dumping was only allowed at certain times and the ship would pipe through the Tannoy when it was authorised to do so as any debris could very easily be absorbed into the engines of the aircraft, and possibly cause a crash and/or death. Waste from the MCO was taken to an onboard incinerator and destroyed. One evening, during flying stations, one of the guys was asked to take the confidential waste from the MCO to be incinerated, but he mis-took the order and decided to ditch it all overboard. Not realising that flying was taking place, he tossed a couple of bags overboard, but the wind carried the bags towards a flying Sea-king helicopter. The paper bags were ripped apart by the down-draught which sent paper and telex tapes flying across the flight deck, much to everyone's horror. The pursuing investigation managed to get Noddy into so much trouble. Luckily, no one was hurt and no aircraft was damaged – although it was grounded for a while to clear out the air intakes. We will never know if our Ruskie friends discovered anything of interest in the sea.

One of the big changes for the Communications team, was that the ship was now fitted with a system for satellite communications for voice and message traffic. A new office-segment was added to the superstructure, adjacent to the flag deck, which was the satellite control room. This was the first sea-trials for the Royal Navy so it was a fabulous introduction to the latest in communications infrastructure. The early UK Military satcom systems called SkyNet-1 were not very successful as both satellites failed however, the UK launched follow-up systems (SkyNet-2) and became the leading of military satcom systems, initially managed by the RAF hosted at RAF Oakhanger (with a second ground station in Cyprus). These satellites were placed into geostationary orbit, which means they are placed exactly 22,236 miles above the equator so, as the earth itself moves round in its own orbit, the satellite moves at the same speed – hence geo-stationary. (note: the geostationary concept was first discussed by Arthur C. Clarke in the 1940s but it took quite a while for this to become reality). Once the signal was 'locked on' we had [almost] perfect conditions for sending/receiving signal traffic BUT, the ship had to steer in the same compass-direction during transmission else the signal was lost. This caused all kinds of drop-out problems but it proved to be a much better solution than HF wire antennae and relying on the bounce-effect. I did get to work with some of the world's leading Satellite Communications companies again later in my civilian career, and learned how to overcome these problems with navigational GPS Maritime, with a simple modification which became standard in all sea-going systems.

One of the most impressive sights that the Royal Navy are so good at, is the replenishment at sea (RAS) and Ark Royal with her RFA supply vessels always provided a very well-rehearsed operation. This involves the two (or more) ships, heading in the same direction, at the same speed and with just a few metres between them. Lines are sent across between the ships and a full replenishment begins. Ark Royal could refuel from two lines on the starboard side, and take stores from the port side, and do continuous helicopter drops at the same time. RFA Olwen (A122) was often sent to keep Ark Royal going; she was an Ol-class fleet tanker (with sister ships Olna A123 and Olmeda A124) which could simultaneously refuel two warships - a spectacular capability.

When taking on stores during RAS, it was the duty of all the ships company to assist with the loading (except those watchkeepers required in their 'day jobs'). I always tried to get into my favoured position, on a stairway down to the food freezers where we would man-handle the stores from man-to-man (hand-to-hand) down the ladders and into the store. I liked to stand just outside the Chogey Laundrymen's messdeck, as they would often pop out to see what was going on and where you could negotiate a missing box (or two), in return for a can (or three). One box of frozen pork chops equals six cans of beer. A good trade we thought, and helped the RAS speed along unhindered.

So, more sea training, more watching soviets, more exercises, more flying – and the Ark Royal was about to make brief stops in Puerto Rico meaning another inevitable visit to the Black Angus Club; to Bridgetown Barbados, where we discovered a new club venue "Harry's Nighterie" offering live on-stage scantily-clad dancing girls, fun and frolics, but also an introduction for young Willy Mac to the infamous New York bar and the queue of buckets. We did manage a return to the fabulous Everglades, Disney and the glorious beaches of Fort Lauderdale, and finally another trip to the US Navy Base Norfolk, Virginia.

I was now scheduled to leave Ark Royal after two fantastic years onboard, but there was one more thing I had to do before I left. I paid a visit to K.P. Lau's tailor shop and ordered a made-to-measure suit. I don't know why exactly, but I chose a Prince of Wales check which sounded great at the time. I had never owned a suit before so I was going in at the deep end and buying made to measure. The team were great, and in just two days, the suit was ready for fitting. I thought I looked the bees-knees so I was going to wear this back home to Winchester. There was one small problem though – I didn't have any civvy shoes so ended up wearing my smart new suit and a pair of Doc Marten boots!

I left HMS Ark Royal in May 1975, flying crab-air (RAF) from US Navy Base in Norfolk VA back the UK at RAF Brize Norton. This was my first time flying and I was a little excited about the experience. We landed in the UK and were taken to the railway station, where Joey and I managed to start the journey home, he was headed to Guildford and had a giant Winnie-the-Pooh to carry – a gift for his girlfriend. By the time we reached Reading, the last trains had already left, so we headed to the local police station and asked if we could stay there for the night. We stayed awake and chatted most of the night, not realising at the time as best Ark Royal mates, we would never see each other again! Up early next morning and excited to be going home again but sad to be leaving behind such great memories and experiences.

In some ways I was a little annoyed that I would miss out on the next part of Ark Royal's travels as she too left Norfolk and sailed south to Rio de Janeiro in Brazil – very envious. HMS Ark Royal and many of my messmates from 5K1 did go on to make a major BBC documentary series 'Sailor', showing life on board the ship during a February to July 1976 Western Atlantic deployment. Her Skipper at this time was Captain Wilfred Graham, and the ship's Commander David Cowling. The theme tune for the programme was 'Sailing' by Rod Stewart – a song that came to be associated with the ship and her successor.

HMS Ark Royal's career spanned just 24 years from the time of her commissioning (her name became a household word), she spent as much time in refit, repair and modernisation as in commissioned service. The scrapping of Ark Royal in 1979 marked the end of conventional fixed-wing aircraft operations aboard Royal Navy carriers. She had such a fearsome presence as a British warship and had borne so many innovations, yet her replacement (Ark Royal V) was not equipped with any of these. Yes indeed, I was heading back to HMS Mercury to attend a training course for LRO (Leading Radio Operator) so was excited about that too – or so I thought!

9. MERCURY, A REUNION AND A MAGICAL LOAN

In many ways it was nice to be back at dear old HMS Mercury, the place I had spent many months of training, learning, and partying. I registered for duty with the OOW (Officer of the Watch) and was told to report to the Exercise Wireless Office (XWO) on the basement floor of Nelson Block. Once in, I was informed that I was not going to be allocated a space on the LRO course as I was in my last 18 months of service and the cost of the course would be wasted if I left the RN as planned – and there was no point in my attending the training anyway. I was gutted by this decision but it did make sense. Instead, I was given a role within the XWO which would see me through my final months in the service, or so I thought.

Being back close to home was good too, so I did try to make an application for Ration Ashore allowance, and/or Home-to-Duties travel allowance, but as I wasn't married this request was immediately denied. I was allocated accommodation and a bunk space, but still travelled home as often as I could. This was a time to get a motorbike. One of my old school mates, Dinger-Lynchy, was upgrading his motorbike, so selling his old machine. I purchased his Yamaha 125 Twin Sport, a small two-stroke bike to get me between Mercury and Winchester each day. Back in those days the motorcycle part-1 pre-test wasn't invented, so as a novice I simply donned the L-Plates and rode off into the sunset. I did have a couple of near misses, but my biggest struggle was mastering the gear change (1d-4u) from 1 – 2 without revving too high in neutral as I forgot the double-kick-up. I learned the same back roads that my Dad taught me a few years earlier, and on a good day, I was able to get to Mercury in under 30minutes.

As I was now set to be at Mercury for a while, I joined up as a volunteer member of the Mercury Club Committee and starting assisting with the planning social events for the base. The resident DJ was DJ Steve Campion, and others worked the NAAFI bar. The club had a great reputation for creating a number of different events, so Sunday Discos were regular and the extremely popular Folk nights and sing-a-longs with fellow matelot singer Shep Wooley and guests Jasper Carrot (and others). At this time, I recognised someone in the club whom I knew very well – it was the Ganges NAAFI store breaker, Stuckey. Of course, we shared a beer and some long catch-ups, and he introduced me to his girlfriend, a serving 'Jenny' (WRN) RO whom he had planned to marry at some point soon. It wasn't long before he ditched his previously allocated Best Man and appointed me in his place, and before long, we were planning a weekend trip to Middlesbrough for the weeding. But what would I wear as I couldn't see myself at a wedding in a Prince of Wales check Chinese tailored K.P. Lau suit – but luckily, I still had a navy blue pin-striped suit that I had borrowed from Coxall a few years earlier, that would be a much better colour match to the groom. When we arrived, we were accommodated at one of the lad's parents, so no hotels costs, thus headed to the nearest bar in the town. The wedding was a big success and Stuckey and his new wife thanked me, before we headed back south. That was probably the last time I saw Stuckey, at least until we both ended up working at BT in the civvy world in the late 90s.

Back in Mercury the job function of the XWO was a series of fleet training exercises using all methods of telecommunications. Mercury has its own transmission and reception equipment, and similarly the ability to engage with ships at sea via RATT, CW and voice services for training purposes. My first job was to ensure that Morse training transmissions were sent out every day, with differing speeds at pre-set frequencies, at set times throughout the day. Often, we could just set the tape running and leave the machine to do the rest, but occasionally the tape would jam and you had to intervene manually – keying 8x 'e' and reset the tape. An easy job and a little boring at times, but an essential training facility for the fleet at sea. As we had a lot of time on our hands, and added to my disappointment of not being allowed the LRO course, I requested permission to use some time to complete the LRO Provisional exam. Whilst I was never going to get that promotion, I did feel it would give me some sense of personal achievement and comfort that I might have passed the actual course if I had attended. The Chief Sparker agreed, and set up a training programme for me to complete. On 16th September 1975 I passed the LRO(G) Provisional Examination and my training records were updated. I stayed in the XWO for a few more months when the CRS asked me to join him in his office for a chat. He congratulated me on my LRO-Prov exam pass, and told me that HMS Ariadne, a Leander class frigate was about to embark on a tour of the Mediterranean and need a 'loan' Sparker for watchkeeping. This would be a three-month loan with a fixed date return to Mercury at the end. I jumped at the opportunity and had my bags packed in extra quick time. I resigned my place on the Mercury Club committee and raced the motorbike home to Winchester. My Dad took me to Pompey dockyard the next morning.

HMS Ariadne was a very new Leander-class frigate only launched in 1971 and her first commission was just two years earlier in 1973. She was the last of the Leander class to be built and like all the others in the class, named after a Greek mythology character – allegedly, Ariadne was the Greek goddess of labyrinths and passions! Once onboard I met with Paul 'Ben' Cartwright, also a two-star RO1(G) who was to become my watchkeeping partner for the tour. We quickly established a good basis for 'who would do what' within our watch. Ben was particularly good at the ICS C&M desk so did most of the transmitter tuning, and he loved to claim the seat at the Killick-of-the-Watch desk in the MCO. Once settled, we sailed south toward Gibraltar as the first scheduled stop. Ariadne was not involved in many exercises as this as going to mainly be a Royal Navy flag-waving tour, with the US Navy in tow, on a clockwise tour around the Mediterranean stopping at Gibraltar, Nice (France), Naples (Italy), Cagliari (Sardinia), Taranto (Italy), Athens (Greece), Izmir (Turkey), Malta and back to Portsmouth via Gibraltar again. There would be some random ship manoeuvres at times, but for the most part it was 'a cruise'.

The tour started so civilised, with a regular stop-over in Gib, and as we had both done the 'tourists' visits before, the inevitable first call was a bar. This visit set the scene for what was going to be a fantastic three-months travelling to new exotic places, new friendships and great experiences.

A beer in Lottie's Bar, Gibraltar

Many of the scheduled stop over places were relatively small, non-commercial ports with lots of privately owned vessels, so the practice of 'Mediterranean mooring' was adopted. Also known as "Med Mooring" this is a technique for mooring a vessel to pier, stern-side on with an anchor dropped at the bow, or tied on to mooring buoys. The ship then occupies less space on the quayside as it is connected to a fixed length of quay along the width rather than the length. The gangway is then applied at the stern of the ship. This took some time for the Americans to master, a few times we saw US sailors in the water, or the ship ram the quayside. The Brit's had it very well rehearsed so no problems from our side.

Nice offered a lovely but very expensive visit. Nice is known for its fantastic climate, fabulous beaches and beautiful coastline with captivating scenery over-looking the Mediterranean. The natural environment of Nice and its mild climate came to the attention of the English upper classes as an alternative to the very exclusive Monte Carlo in the Principality of Monaco, just a short drive north where the world's super-rich can be seen. The city's main seaside promenade, the Promenade des Anglais (translates as Walkway of the English) owes its name to the rich British visitors to the town. The south of France is renowned as a rich people haven, and the place sure lived up to its name in that sense – the cost of eating out, or even having a cold beer on a street lined restaurant, was extortionate. Hence to say, we didn't stay there long.

Next stop Naples was much more to our liking - a city famed for its piazzas, palaces and castles and also Naples is traditionally credited as the home of pizza, and famously, the Margherita pizza was named after Queen Margherita of Savoy after her visit to the city – allegedly! According to popular tradition, during a visit to Naples of the Queen, a chef created a pizza resembling the colours of the Italian flag, red (tomato), white (mozzarella) and green (basil). They named it after the Queen, and is still the most popular pizza today. I loved Italy, the people were so warm, polite and caring, the food was just great and, most of all, we found a few bars that were offering 'free beer' to visiting British sailors. Uh oh!

Ben and I took time to visit a porcelain factory in an attempt to find a capo-de-monte figure or two. I did end up buying a couple of pieces which both had a seal that bears a crown and the signature letter "N" below it. This letter [allegedly] stands for 'Neapolitan,' which is a mark of high-quality from the Royal Factory in Naples – but (I think) they're not the real thing. My Mum still has these to this day. The next day, we took a bus trip to Pompeii the ancient Roman city that was destroyed by the (still active) volcano, Mount Vesuvius. Pompeii, along with the village of Herculaneum and many villas in the surrounding area was buried under 20ft of volcanic ash during the eruption. Much of the city has now been excavated to uncover a small snapshot of Roman life, frozen at the moment it was buried. This was an education for both of us, and something to chat about on the bus back. That evening we headed to a bar, but found ourselves in a back-street market. There were some interesting stalls selling the usual tourist tat, but at one stall, we found some athletic starting pistols with .22 blank cartridges. I think the ADHD kicked in at this point, or maybe it was a combination of that and the alcohol, as we imagined ourselves as John Steed from the TV series The Avengers, and we started shooting at each other, rolling on the ground and across the bonnets of cars. When I think of this today, we were lucky we didn't get shot or locked up for real!

Next stop was Cagliari, and the first time we were med-moored alongside an American warship. Cagliari is the capital city of the Italian island of Sardinia known for the famous hilltop Castle, a medieval walled city looking over the new town. The two ships had agreed to have a series of sailor swaps where we had an opportunity to see how the yanks worked. I had done this previously on the USS JFK, so I left it to Ben to take advantage of their hospitality. When a visiting sailor comes into your own messdeck, it is a RN tradition that each person offers a can of beer to the visitor. Our US colleague was so overwhelmed, he eventually stopped refusing beer and started drinking, but with just a few cans in, he was well on the way to alcohol heaven. He said that he liked english beer, but it was far too strong for him, so he eventually stopped drinking. He suggested that Ben and I met him that evening so he could take us to a local bar to repay the compliment – we agreed. That evening, as we left the ship, the yank was standing waiting for us. First stop, the nearest bar where he purchased a bottle of Seagram's VO Canadian Whisky. I had not heard of this particular brand, but the yank suggested it was great and poured three large glasses. We sat for a while and chatted about everything and nothing, but Ben noticed that whilst we were drinking, the yank wasn't – he was still quite pissed from his time onboard HMS Ariadne earlier that afternoon and I think, the glass of whiskey just finished him off. He apologised to us for letting the side down (?) he handed us the bottle of whisky and a large wad of US Dollars, and told us to have a night out on him. He left the bar and went back to his ship. Wow! That was a great cheap night out for us as we headed off into town.

Next stop was back on the Italian mainland - Taranto has a naturally deep harbour which made it a logical home port for the Italian naval fleet since before and during the First World War. During World War II, Taranto became famous for a November 1940 British air attack on the Marina and Naval base stationed here, which is recorded in history as the Battle of Taranto. The story of our time there was similar to the previous stops – a little blurred by beer, although Taranto was a military port so the drinking was a little more contained as our British-ness took over.

Next was much better - Athens - the capital of Greece. It is also right at the centre of Ancient Greek mythology which has been discussed for centuries. The city is still dominated by 5th-century BC landmark the Acropolis, a hilltop citadel topped with ancient buildings and the famous Parthenon temple. The Parthenon is a former temple on the Acropolis, Greece, dedicated to the goddess Athena, whom the people of Athens considered their patron. Whenever someone talks of Greece, the symbol of the Parthenon usually pops into one's mind. This tour continues to be a big blur fuelled by alcohol and I'm sure there are many stories that are yet to be revealed. I did meet up with Ben again very briefly in 2019, but a full reunion is yet to be arranged.

Back onboard and our last port of call was Malta. One of the guys onboard was particularly looking forward to this visit as he had planned to meet up with his brother. When I discovered his surname was Marshall, it reminded me of a Bunting whom I served with back onboard HMS Ark Royal. A brief chat confirmed that this same guy was now serving in Communications Centre (ComCen) Malta and I was now serving on Ariadne with his younger brother. With a reputation as a drinker, we were in for a great night on the town to celebrate this family reunion.

So, the loan draft and mini-tour of the Med had ended and I was now heading back to HMS Mercury for a reunion of my own and many more sea-stories of exotic travel over a pint with mates at the Mercury club, and valuable time with my family back in in Winchester. Once again, my sister had arranged yet another date for me, this time with her friend Denise. The date didn't last long as Denise was definitely a candidate for the mess gronk board.

10. ROYAL NAVY DISPLAY TEAM

The Ariadne loan well and truly put to bed; I was back on terra firma and back at HMS Mercury. I was hoping to also be back into my place at the XWO but discovered that I had been replaced during my absence and I was now moving into the Security Team. This was going to be boring and I wasn't looking forward to the change. The main thrust of the job as a NP (Naval Patrol) so day-time was spent sitting at the door of every main building, checking security ID cards of all who entered, and night time was patrolling the base with torch and pick-axe handle. Not a very exhilarating job and a complete waste of my training. Of course, we tried to make the most of what we had been dealt, and looked for ways to entertain ourselves whilst being bored out of our skulls. My ADHD was perfect for this, so I was constantly trying to engineer some excitement – I had a brilliant history of inadvertently getting into trouble and was good at being stupid, too. The problem was, this crap job got the better of me and the ADHD or ADD transformed itself into 'arrogance', and I hated almost everything and everyone and developed some anger issues.

I spent a lot of time at home and trying to watch the occasional Saints FC game, although tickets were hard to get and my brother Mick was now dating too, so my ticket source was drying up. The new manager at Saints Lawrie

McMenemy was doing very well and his new team provided a good mix of senior and junior players, and were on a great FA Cup run. Some new players included big centre half David Peach who, working alongside Jim Steele provided a very strong back line and our own youngster Bobby Stokes was delivering some excellent displays up front. Backed by a brilliant midfield pair of Channon and Osgood, this could be the year we were going to get out of Division-2.

A decision that for some reason, still baffles me today; I traded in my Yamaha 125 for a Honda 175, I think this decision was driven by an assumption the extra cc on the engine might mean a faster ride, but I soon discovered that the bike was actually slower. The new bike was tolerable, but it did start to play up. My brother Mick came to recover me and the bike a few times in his truck. I eventually persuaded my Dad to be a guarantor for me, and I took out a hire purchase agreement and upgraded to Honda CB250, a much more powerful machine which got me back to Mercury easily. My brother Mick also gave me an old scooter that he had acquired from somewhere, a Lambretta LI 250 which he had already resprayed the side panels to a bright orange colour – I think it was free paint from his workplace and he was practicing his spraying techniques. The Lambretta was fun too, but the Honda CB250 was a much better ride all-round.

Back at the HMS Mercury NP duty - the last job of the night-watch was to clean the accommodation block and bathrooms. One morning it was my turn for this laborious task, so I went off, mopped the bathroom floors then lay on my bed waiting for the time to pass. Back in those days, BBC Radio-1 didn't start transmitting until 7am, so I set up my mini-transistor radio, pre-tuned ready for 7am. Laying on the bed was a mistake, as I simply fell asleep so when the radio started blaring, I was already well into the land of nod. The pursuing racket woke up the other watchkeepers who all sprang into life and started shouting and screaming at me. I apologised, switched off the radio and got on with the task in hand. Later that day, Jack Frost, one of the boys, reported the early morning fuss to the PO i/c and I was sent to the

Commanders table. I received 7 days No9s punishment for the incident, which was a little embarrassing being the only 'senior' on No9s amongst lots of Juniors still in initial training. Another reason to hate everything and a beer you still owe me, Mr Frost!

After a few months of sheer boredom, I was drafted yet again; I was heading of back to Portsmouth to HMS Vernon, a former minesweeper base, to join up with the Royal Navy Display Team 1976. I was now well into my final 6 months in the service, and this draft was so awful, it just reminded me how happy I was to be leaving. It was a shame really; if I had made a different decision about signing-on for more years, I (might) have been drafted to something more interesting, or even got my LRO and drafted back to sea. Ho hum! I was able to ride the new motorbike to Portsmouth, and take the bike into the barracks which offered a little relief. I was about to become a window ladder gymnast and a field gun runner. Oh goody! (*sarcastic*).

The first morning, we lined up on parade and were told to get into PT kit. Our introduction to the RNDT was a long jog from Vernon barracks, down to the seafront in Southsea, a jog up and back along the stoney beach, and then back to base. Have you ever tried running on a stoney beach? I was forced to stop a few times along the way to cough and splutter (and cough some more) and was completely unfit and exhausted by the time we got back. The POPTI suggested this would be a normal start to every day until we were all fit for the gymnastics displays, we would be performing around the country. The morning runs did get better, but a few weeks in, I just popped to the toilet before the parade, and when I returned, the gang had already left. I had accidently discovered a way out of the morning run and shared it with a few others. I did also bump into a guy who I served with at HMS Ganges who was in his second term in the RNDT. 'Beardsley' was there to provide continuity across the team change. I think it was him who 'volunteered' me as a potential window ladder climber.

My arrogant attitude was taking a strong hold as I really didn't want to be doing this. We started training on the window ladder climbing routine, each movement by numbers, then each movement with accompanying music. Once we had mastered all movements, it was time to start practicing how to carry the frame, and how to assemble it on a parade ground, or onto a military tattoo event arena. The display culminates with the four different ways to exit the routine by rope. I was in the second row to climb, so the third to descend: the first row descent was the traditional hand-over-hand; second descent was using two ropes, and hands free; third (my descent) was hand-over-hand upside down; with the final row upside down, no hands. It took a while to get this right, but there were no incidents or injuries.

The second part of the RNDT was the field gun run – now just to confirm, this is not the full-time Command Team running you might see at the Royal Tournament, but a version of that with the same heavy equipment. I had competed in a smaller junior version of this at HMS Ganges, but now we were on to the heavier guns and limber trucks. Once we had the basics together, it was just a case of rehearse, rehearse and rehearse again, just to reduce the time to make it competitive. We were soon ready for the road and off on tour around the UK seeking regional country shows and the odd military tattoo. First stop was the Birmingham Tulip festival – yup! Oh dear, this was really going to be an exciting draft! We performed the window ladder and the field gun, and after the show, had to rush back to the coaches and change into full No1 uniform, grab a SLR to provide a military guard for the visiting dignitaries. The show went down well with the crowds and provided us a good full-dress rehearsal for the next show.

We were now ready for the real thing, and was heading over to Belgium to provide a display at a military music festival. The travelling team was two trucks, a Bedford flatbed and a pantechnicon (shortened to pantec, truck) plus two coaches and civvy drivers hired from National Express. We headed off to Felixstowe and ferried to Zeebrugge for the road trip into the country. We were to be billeted in an old army camp, which was cold and dirty, but after such a long road journey, were given the night off. A couple of the lads, Jessie James, Scouse, Paddy Lynch and I headed into town to sample the local brew, and our first experience of Belgium beer was not a good one. On our way back to barracks, Jessie and I saw the town were flying flags so tried to climb onto a bridge to take one down, but this resulted in him being arrested by the local police. I tried to plea-bargain for his release but ended up in the police cells myself. The two of us were finally released early the following morning - without charges, albeit setting the agenda for my own reputation throughout the coming months. The show itself was not really a thing for us climbers, but we did our display to a good applause, and the field guns were there merely to provide some loud 'bangs' and smoke during a performance of Tchaikovsky's 1812 Overture.

By now the show programme had really taken off and we were booked for the Edinburgh Tattoo, also to be screened live on the BBC; as well as that, we managed to get a place on live Children's ITV for the show 'Runaround' hosted by TV Comedian Mike Reid. But first we had a few more appointments around the country; a military tattoo in Congleton; a country show in Whitehaven and another hosted by ourselves in Portsmouth.

Whilst I was training hard and working the show, Southampton FC were on a fantastic FA Cup run and had made it to the final at Wembley to take on the mighty Manchester United. In one of the biggest shocks in the history of the final, Division-2 Southampton won 1–0 through an 83rd-minute goal from Bobby Stokes. It was the first time Southampton won a major trophy, and the last time that the Queen attended a final and presented the trophy to the winners. Fortunately, I did get to see some of the game on TV, and then able to get home to Winchester the following day. My return to Portsmouth barracks was an interesting one as I flew red and white ribbons from the back of my motorbike amongst a lot of shouting and abuse as I rode through the streets on my way back to Vernon barracks. Who cared – my team had just won the FA Cup!

There was a very brief moment of pride when in June of 1976, Her Majesty the Queen was to host a state visit by the French President and the Royal Navy was tasked with providing the street lining effect in London. The RNDT were deployed to HMS Excellent, the fleet gunnery school on Whale Island, to meet with some heavy-duty GIs who would teach us the street lining routine. This meant a whole week of drill with rifles. You might recall that 1976 was one of the hottest summers on record, and we were practicing street lining, in full No1 dress uniform in the blistering heat. On the day prior to the parade, we headed off to London and stayed a night in the old billet rooms of the Union Jack Club in Waterloo. The following morning, we dressed in our best No1 uniforms with added white gloves, belt and gaiters and started the march toward Victoria station. We collected our SLR rifles and started our march into place, whilst the

Queen drove by in her coach and escort, to collect the French president from the station. This meant standing at ease, or at attention, and a Royal Salute in both directions before we could march back to the guard's barracks at Birdcage Walk. It was indeed a proud moment and for once, I was happy to be there to witness the Queen's brief drive-pass and feel first hand, what it like for those Guardsman who do this every week. Whilst back at the barracks, an RSM Guardsman came out of the building and starting shouting orders at the Grenadiers – we just all laughed because we couldn't understand what it was all about, but the RSM in his split-peak forage cap almost flat on his face, wasn't too happy with us and charged over to our platoon. He said something about 'mamby-pamby' sailors and left us alone.

The coach trip to Whitehaven in Cumbria was long and arduous and when we arrived, we learned we were to be billeted in a primary school, on camp beds. Well, this was awful – no decent washrooms, no showers and nowhere to cook food - just a boring school hall. We did manage to find a record player but only one single record – Russ Conway playing 'Side Saddle' on his piano, which was played over-and-over until everyone was sick of it. The display was the Cumbria County Agricultural Show, so no real military connection. We did have fun walking around the showground after our performance, and bumped into a couple of nurses who were on their day out. One of the girls was getting married the next day, so invited us to her wedding reception at the West Cumberland Hospital. On arrival, it seemed strange that we were gate-crashing a wedding, but enjoyed the evening, free bar and a great buffet – we even provided an impromptu alcohol-fuelled song and dance act on the stage, for free. We had a fabulous evening and met so many of the bride's family. We'll never know what the groom thought of all the shenanigans. That night was spent at the hospital where we managed to get rooms at the nurse's home.

The next display was at Congleton Park, but we were stayed at RAF Stafford, so had to be shipped back and forth each day for the rehearsals and the show itself. It was only a weekend show so two days maximum stay at the RAF camp, however we spent much of this time in the NAAFI club. Again, there wasn't much of a military connection with the town of Congleton, so the show was just in support of its annual park event on the council's calendar. This weekend was to get me into trouble yet again, as I and a couple of the lads met up with a group of girls whom we spent the afternoon chatting with. This ended up with a couple of the girls asking if they could scrounge a lift with us, to Stafford. Later that evening, the two of them were smuggled her onto our coach where I hid one of them under my seat, and then into the RAF base. That evening, as we went into the NAAFI bar, the two of them were drinking and sharing a laugh with all the guys; they eventually disappeared so I assumed they had gone off with someone or even gone home. The next day we went into Congleton for the show, and upon return to barracks, the RAF police, and the Civvy police were waiting for the bus. They came onboard and shouted my name – "Willis, come here". I was taken to the guardroom and asked about one of the missing girls, and I explained that I did sneak her into the camp, but didn't see them again after we left the bar. I was then taken to Stafford Police station for more discussions, I learned that the girl whom was with me, was an under-aged runaway, reported missing by her family. The two girls were found the next day and returned home and I was charged with "bringing an unauthorised person onto a military base" by the RAF – which meant, (you know it) 7 days No9s punishment once back at Portsmouth. I did get a request to attend a meeting with a Chief Inspector at Portsmouth Police station who warned me of the dangerous consequences if this had gone further. I had no idea that she was a runaway, and certainly no perception that she might be underage. A very close call and a valuable life lesson learned. By the way POPTI 'Joe' – that's a pint you still owe me too!

We were now on the way to Scotland to perform at the Royal Edinburgh Tattoo. We were billeted at Glencorse Barracks, a British Army unit situated just outside the town of Penicuik in Midlothian, but the accommodation was, once again, pretty poor. Most of the Tattoo entertainers were located there, so we were able to mix socially with the Pongos of several regiments, and with the Royal Gurkha regiment. The Tattoo performance took place every weekday evening and twice on Saturdays throughout August so we had a tough schedule coming up. The rehearsals were every morning before the castle was opened to the general public, so early start and a training performance before breakfast. Our social evenings didn't really happen as by the time the evening performance had completed, it was a struggle to get back to barracks before the NAAFI bar closed at 10:30pm. On the last night, we did take over the bar completely as one of the lads organised some dancers/strippers to provide some light entertainment before we headed back down south.

Edinburgh was a tough challenge in the extremely hot 1976 summer weather and displaying our skills every day for the month of August certainly took its toll on us. We did get some time off to explore the city, but for the most part, we kept ourselves to ourselves. On one outing, I noticed that the local off-licence was selling cider at a reduced rate, so a box of 12 bottles was less than £5 – a temptation too much for me. I took the offer, but was very sure NOT to drink before the performance that evening. The CPO in charge kept asking me if I had been drinking, but he didn't believe me when I told him no, so kept asking again and again. Eventually, I took his challenge and pretended to be drunk – so he sent an army medical doctor over to test me – touch your nose, touch my finger, touch your nose – touch my finger – all that rubbish. Of course, I hadn't been drinking as it would have been dangerous and foolish if I had. The Chief eventually believed me nevertheless, I was still taken off the climbing team for the final performance at Portsmouth, but by then then I was really into my run-down period (RDP) and had just a few weeks left to serve.

RNDT76 finished with a team party at the Blue Lagoon club near Hilsea Lido but I had been on leave for a long weekend prior. During this time, I intentionally started to grow a moustache just to demonstrate my arrogance and the banter, and to see what the Divisional Officer, and the CPO might say. Technically, I was still a serving RN rating so was another final stint of No9s coming my way again, but they simply dismissed me as a 'civvy idiot' and nothing more was said.

11. BACK TO CIVVY LIFE

After leaving Vernon barracks and the RNDT for the last time, I was excited to be leaving the Royal Navy too. I had already invested a lot of time and telephone calls back home, chasing the civvy job market in and around Winchester. The RN owed me 15 days termination leave and I had no intention of wasting any of it. I was keen to stay with what I knew well – radio systems and communications, so I was interested in anything within this genre. I was about to embark on my final ship – named citizen-ship, and was looking forward to entering that massive cavern on the other side of the port hole, called civilian street. Initially, I explored an opportunity with the Hampshire Police in their headquarters building, for a position as control room staff, but this didn't happen. One evening I was chatting to my Dad who saw a very small two-line advertisement in the Hampshire Chronicle, the local newspaper – it simply read "Trainee Computer Operator required, shift work, no experience necessary". My Dad suggested I gave them a call to see what this was about, so after a discussion about what I knew about computers, he reminded me that the Ad said "no experience necessary". What did I have to lose? I made the call, spoke to a lovely lady in the Personnel department of the Independent Broadcasting Authority, which ended with her inviting me to attend an interview the following week. She would confirm in writing. The IBA was the UK regulatory body for all commercial television (ITV and later Ch4/Ch5) and commercial Independent Local Radio (ILR). The interview was to be with the Computer Operations Manager at their new Engineering headquarters in Crawley, a small village near Winchester. On the day, I donned my best K. P. Lau Chinese tailored suit, hopped on my motorbike and headed to Crawley all very nervous as this was my first 'real' job interview. On arrival, I met Mr Brady and Mr Hale, and we chatted for about 45minutes. He explained to me that he had received over 60 applicants for the position, but I was on the shortlist of five, so I should be very pleased with that. He then launched many questions about my time serving onboard warships in the RN and after a short while, told me that he was also former military - an ex-RAF signals sergeant. From then on, we established a great rapport and the rest of the interview seemed to fly by. I explained that I was now a free agent and was available to start at any time. I then met with the lady from Personnel whom I spoken with on the telephone – her name was Gloria and again the rapport was very good - I was gaining more confidence as the meeting went on. Two hours later I left the building, they both thanked me for my time saying, "we'll be in touch". I went home excited to tell Mum and Dad what had happened. Later that same evening, I received a telephone call from Gloria saying that I was successful and could I be available the following Monday. Wow! I explained again that I was on termination leave from the RN and needed two days off the end of the month to visit HMS Nelson in Portsmouth, to return my kit and finally sign off from the RN. They agreed, and I started my initial shift the following week. My first Civvy job interview went down a storm I was about to embark on a completely fantastic new chapter of my life.

I should just mention here, that later in 1982, whilst working at the IBA, Argentina made military advances and illegally invaded British Sovereign Territory and sent thousands of their troops into the Falkland Islands. The conflict began in April, when Argentina invaded the islands, followed by an invasion of South Georgia the very next day.

The British Government took a series of military decisions to recapture the islands and the British inhabitants from the Argentines and so ordered the Royal Navy toward the south Atlantic. A task force was assembled and sent to engage. The UK was ready to fight and many of our best forces were now on their way south, including the Royal Marines and the Parachute Regiments, and I'm sure the Special Air Service were already there by now just watching and learning. As the UK was preparing to recall reservists, I called the RN careers office in Southampton and asked if volunteers were being considered. In between giggles, there was a serious suggestion that I might be able to free up capable reservists to go south, and I might consider enlisting with the Territorial Army. I did this, and enquired about linking up with 233 Squadron RCT, part of 155 Transport Regiment, Royal Corps of Transport, based in Southampton. When I arrived for my interview with Captain Tom, the drill hall was laid out with camp beds and full of Army personnel headed for the Falkland's, all loaded with equipment and ready to depart. I was accepted into the TA, but of course, I was never destined to go down to the south Atlantic and the war was well and truly over before I could even get on an Army recruit's course. The TA did offer a few other benefits though; I passed driving tests in HGV3, HGV2 and Motorcycle, and embarked on a rapid promotion to Sergeant based on my previous RN experience and my vast knowledge of radio communications systems and antennae. I then went on to set-up 233 Sqn Signals section to become the top Sigs troop in the Regiment. This was a great achievement and helped me get enlisted onto a Regimental Signals Instructors (RSI) training course, which I passed and awarded the RSI rated cross flags trade badge – oh what would my ex-Navy bunting mates think of this! As part of the UK Mobile Force (UKMF) under NATO command, we had some fabulous exercise duties in Germany and Denmark over the years. It did seem a little strange that I bumped into a familiar face, Bungy Edwards – a guy I joined the RN with back in the 70s at HMS Ganges. He too had the same feelings as me (or did he just want the HGV?) but he was now serving in the same squadron, in the 'A' troop at Weymouth barracks. There was a theory that I could earn £26/day as a Sergeant and also be able to get some civvy HGV contract driving jobs to top up the coffers at home.

Later, I managed to get a posting into the regimental Recruit Reception and Training Team (RRTT) where I joined together with WO1 BrianN, Sgt PTI JohnY and a lovely medic Sgt Penelope WRAC. I later took over the PTI role when John retired so I tried to employ some of the RN PTI tactics that I was pushed so hard on, when I was a matelot. The Falklands War was now a distant memory, but I enjoyed the Army so much, I stayed with them for over 9 years.

There is absolutely no doubt that the skills and techniques learned in the Royal Navy (and maybe some from the Army) helped me pass the City & Guilds examinations in Electronics to become a licensed Radio Amateur callsign Golf-Zero-India-Oscar-Oscar, registered with OfCom, and earned a brief re-introduction to the Royal Navy through the acclaimed RN Amateur Radio Society (RNARS Member 3287). It gave me the basic skills to build wire and mobile antennae for the fabulous world of Citizens Band (CB) radio which was a fad in the late 70s and 80s where I became Chair of the Eastleigh Playpen CB Association for a short while.

Now retired, I have spent the final years of my civilian

working career experiencing senior leadership roles across the IT industry, working with large corporate leaders and helping small start-ups, deliver international IT and Communications Services. The superior Royal Naval training at Ganges and Mercury, and the life experiences learned from my time on Ark Royal, Ariadne (and even the RNDT) had set-up my civvy career for life. On the technology side of things – Teleprinters became visual display units (VDUs) - RATT transmission became 'Data transmission' – TTVFs into Modems – where FSK became just another network protocol - HF Radio, just another data transport mechanism – 75baud was superseded by Gigabit high-speed data transfer – UHF/VHF Voice became Cellular or VoIP – and where 'broadband' in today's world has a completely different meaning and operates at Millions of bits per second (Mbit/s). Many people today know a lot about technology, but still get confused between the simple concept of 'memory' and 'storage' on their mobile phones, and many really don't understand that Bluetooth, Satellite TV and Wi-fi each remain 'just another radio frequency' and the basics are the same.

My civilian career development has been crowned with several professional achievements: I am a Chartered IT Professional (CITP) registered with the Chartered Institute for IT (British Computer Society) and hold full BCS membership (MBCS); I am a member of the Institution of Engineering & Technology (MIET); and I hold a formal Project Management accreditation with APM, the Chartered Body for Project Management (MAPM).

My (still) undiagnosed ADHD is (almost) gone – or has it merely morphed itself into obsessive-compulsive disorder (OCD) type of anxiety disorder where I have recurring, ideas or obsessions that make me feel I have to do something immediately. My wife often says "if it's in your head, you feel you just have to do it now" - but this is our own diagnosis. Some of the classic ADHD symptoms often return; inattentiveness; trouble listening when others are speaking; frequently interrupting; making silly mistakes (related to a desire to get the task finished quickly); restlessness; having difficulty waiting my turn or just not doing something because it's too long. Maybe as I got older, I have learned to manage the poor situations better and not let myself be distracted by other things that, at the time, seem more interesting or more daring. I would sometimes get stressed over work or the kids, but my wife has quickly become an excellent remedy for me in these situations – if I ever get emotionally down, distracted or about to make bad decisions, she would take over and make me see the issue from a different angle, think again, or just make a cup of tea and provide that calming, caring Irish nature. She has a magical ability to calm any nerves, stop any sign of my shaky hands or stammering over my words, to help me kick away any bad thoughts and make me smile. I'm not sure if it was my years in the Royal Navy, that we now laugh at the undiagnosed OCD - I like to have everything in the house clean, tidy, lined up in a straight line, or symmetrical – or as the old Navy saying goes 'all stowed away shipshape and Bristol fashion'.

In 1976, I left my dream job with the Royal Navy, sailing around the world serving Her Majesty the Queen; working through the Cold War and being constantly observed by the Soviets. I learned so much and travelled far and wide, even though the cultural side of my travels was often blurred by beer. In an interesting survey by a RN Veterans social media site, when asked "what was your biggest regrets", almost 90% of respondents said they left the RN too early. With hindsight, I may have left too early, but my civilian career was about to take off – big time!

In 1989, I left my dream job operating a mainframe computer system in independent television and radio broadcast engineering. I learned so much about transferring my RN skills into 'IT speak' and remembering the old radio ways could be easily translated into IT Network terminology without much work.

In 1990, I left my dream job as a Network Support Consultant working for the ITV contractor TVS Television where I was able to develop my computer networking skills and learn new skills on Mainframe-to-PC connectivity and data transfer.

In 1994, I left my dream job as a telecommunications analyst, investigating the best methodology to implement communications systems in some far-out remote sites, then designing and installing satellite networks on maritime vessels and fixed-earth stations, or building HF x25 packet-radio telecommunications systems with copper- wire antennae, around Europe, north and west Africa and Russia, for a major global oil-field services company.

In 1997, I left my dream job as Group Head of Network Services and my first position managing a business process outsource partner, providing local and wide-area network services for a Financial Services company.

In 2004, I left my dream job as Head of IT Infrastructure and my first big people-management break leading an IT Support Services team of over 125 technicians, for the largest and most diverse telecommunications brand in the UK.

In 2006, I left my dream job as Director of Data Centre Services for a major European networking and IT Services company managing several Data Centre installations across Northern Europe.

In 2009, I left my dream job as Director of Data Centre Operations for a major UK and European Satellite Television Networking and Telecommunications brand.

In 2011, I completed a dream 12-month contract as General Manager of Data Centre Services for a major UK and European IT Services and Support company, which briefly took me back to an ex-Royal Navy Officers Mess and now dis-used, Communications Centre at Mountwise, Plymouth as potential purchase target as a Data Centre. We didn't buy it!

In 2012, I left my dream job as Director of IT for a Global Web hosting and Domain name Brand leading a team of specialist technicians hosting internet web services for some well-known UK brands.

In 2014, I left my dream job as Director Platform Operations helping a small German start-up stamp its place as a global presence in a competitive world of device management and web analytics.

In 2016, I left my dream job as Global Head of IT Infrastructure for £3.5Bn Japanese owned Global Media Communications giant, where the work and my senior leadership role took me to across Europe, India, China and the US.

In 2017, I realised that I'd had enough of listening to silly ideas and trying to manage other people's failures. I was tired of listening to corporate bollocks and being foul-mouthed by seniors. I had developed a complete intolerance of idiots - so walked away from a high-salary job simply because...

TODAY? I'm very happy, healthy and living the dream as 'retired' (and an occasional Social Media volunteer for my wife's Irish Dance Academy) and a part-time voluntary school Governor.

I often reflect on my time with the Navy and wear my Armed Services Veterans badge with pride. When I look back, I still believe that the strict discipline was (and still is) a necessity of life for young people, as much as they despise it today. I still spend time with Coxall and Stuckey whom I met up with at HMS Ganges all those years ago. I have joined up with some of the guys I served with onboard HMS Ark Royal (R09) Communications branch, and have had a chance to meet with Fred and Knocker White, two guys who were in 5k1 mess when I joined, and many others who joined whilst I was onboard, and after I left too. We have an annual reunion, swing some lamps and the banter remains as it was way back then, which under the modern agenda, probably not as politically correct as we should be, but when old boys reminisce over the good ole days in the early 70s, the banter makes remembering the 'old days' really worth it. I have continued membership of the Royal Naval Association (RNA) and the Royal Navy Communications Association (RNCA) whom allow me to represent them each November, when I march at the Whitehall Cenotaph in London on Remembrance Day, parading my Dad's RN Suez Crisis medal and ironically, marching alongside an ex-Ark Royal buddy who is guilty of taking me on my very first run ashore in Gibraltar.

I now manage the ADHD well and with age, I have become quite opinionated (wouldn't it be really boring if everyone had the same opinion); I have dropped the arrogance and often consider that my skills in people management are still quite good, but I do have an intolerance of stupid people. My kids are all grown up and are embarking on their own adult lives, but they sometimes criticise and say "you'll speak to anyone Dad" as if it was a strange thing, and I have fantastic grandchildren in tow. In my opinion, my civilian career has been quite successful too – culminating with building, establishing and leading a global-wide IT infrastructure services team to successfully transform and energise a major business – centralising, virtualising and re-platforming IT Services on a global enterprise scale. I have held many senior management, Head and Director 6-figure salaried positions; I have contributed on major international technology innovations and some fairly complex transformation projects. I have experienced first-hand the success of leading IT infrastructure operations, IT Services delivery, Digitalisation and Cloud transformation. All this, and I still have a NAMET 7-6.

If I look back, I wish I could meet up with Mr Green and Mr Starkey, the school careers masters who didn't really care that they wrote me and my future off so easily, or to speak to Mr Beacham the former Headmaster of Montgomery of Alamein school to say "look what I did with my life – and I did all this without you."

I didn't make a few of those work and life changes by choice, but each time, I headed off into a different and an uncertain future, I had the support of my fabulous family, and it always worked out. In my civilian career I have been made redundant twice, I left one job with a compromise agreement and been laid-off twice however, these negatives turned into financial positives allowing my wife and I to pay-off our mortgage 15 years early and the ability to invest in our beautiful holiday home in Co Donegal in the northwest of Ireland. My age may well have slowed me down, but it certainly hasn't shut me up! I always tell people that I no-longer have anger issues – but some people just need to stop pissing me off!

Could I go back to any of the previous jobs? Absolutely not – except maybe the Royal Navy. This proved to the best start to my life that anyone could ever dream of. Would I do that again? Absolutely YES, in a heartbeat.

I was born in Winchester – but made in the Royal Navy.

Dit-dah-dit-dah-dit

ABOUT THE AUTHOR

Alan Willis grew up in a council estate in Winchester with ADHD/ADD (undiagnosed). He found it tough at school and struggled through his youth causing trouble everywhere and ran riot through adolescence and into his skinhead teens. He joined the Royal Navy via HMS Ganges, the tough training establishment for young boys as a very young 15year-old kid. On leaving the senior service, and spending time with the British Army Reserve, he went on to build a successful civilian career spanning 45 years working in the Data Centre and IT Services industry.

Printed in Great Britain
by Amazon